****The****
SAVVY
Student

The
SAVVY
Student

Getting Better Grades Without Working Harder or Being Smarter

PROFESSOR DAVID KINAHAN &
PROFESSOR HARRY HEFT

AVON BOOKS NEW YORK

AVON BOOKS, INC.
1350 Avenue of the Americas
New York, New York 10019

Copyright © 1997 by David Kinahan and Harold Heft
Cover illustration by Greg Stevenson
Inside back cover author photograph by Suzanne Mitchell
Published by arrangement with the authors
ISBN: 0-380-80639-8
Library of Congress Catalog Card Number: 94-94872
www.avonbooks.com

First Avon Books Trade Paperback Printing: August 1999

AVON TRADEMARK REG. U.S. PAT. OFF. AND IN OTHER COUNTRIES, MARCA REGISTRADA,
HECHO EN U.S.A.

Printed in the U.S.A.

OPM   10   9   8   7   6   5   4   3   2   1

* * *

For Ruby, Eddie, Carolyn and Liam,
and all our students who've played us like a violin.

CONTENTS

"[Professors] will seem to you to be lofty and in command of vast quantities of knowledge that you can never possess. But it is time to . . . bring them down from that pedestal."

** The **
SAVVY
Student

INTRODUCTION

I don't mind school . . . as long as it doesn't inter-
fere with my education.

The graffiti over the toilet paper roll tells the tale: "Bachelor's Degrees: please take one." While perhaps things aren't quite this desperate, the market value of a typical undergraduate degree has taken a beating over the last few decades. It used to be that if you earned a college or university degree you were virtually ensured of employment and above-average financial security. Those days are long gone.

Don't get us wrong, your undergraduate degree will still be an important accomplishment and an opportunity for enriching personal development. It is just that trying to make a potential employer acknowledge its virtue is like trying to sell chicken farmers on a particular egg—they've seen a lot of them, so what's so damn special about yours? As a result of this loss of employment clout, it seems that the degree is, more and more, turning into a kind of a preparatory qualification for entrance into other programs—law school, medical school, MBAs, and so on. When we were enrolled in first-year science, nobody in our classes was doing a BS; everyone was pre-med or pre-law, or breaking their back to get into a good chiropractic school.

And now, because you and so many of your classmates aspire to take that next educational step beyond the bachelor's degree, the competition for space in the various professional schools is incredibly fierce. A few percentage points on your transcript can add up to the difference between program acceptance and form-letter rejection, between full scholarships and student-loan repo-men. *The Savvy Student* shows you where those few percentage points are hidden and tells you how best to flush them out, how to convert your C into a B, and how to move yourself from the B range into the land of A. *The Savvy Student* positions you to boost your grades without working any harder.

In this book we focus on your relationship with your professor, and we maintain that the nature of that relationship does much to determine the level of the grades you'll receive. It's not too difficult a formula: If your professors like and respect you, you'll do better in their courses than you will if you are invisible to them or actively disliked by them. The hard part is getting you to that place where you know what to do to become this favored student. And if you think it's about sucking up, then you'd better read on because taking that strategy will have all the success of a vendor trying to sell a hot dog at a vegetarian convention (nobody's going to buy it).

The first step toward understanding how to play your relationship with your professor involves understanding the psychology of your professor. Seemingly encased in an ivory tower and dedicated to the pursuit of the pure intellect, the professor is an intimidating and enigmatic figure to the rookie undergraduate. *The Savvy Student* renders the professor more approachable, and stresses the necessity for you to make that approach to your professors. If you can understand a little more about how the professor sees the system and her work, then you can use that awareness in your contact with her. If you begin to think of your professors as human beings with all the petty annoyances and daily distractions of other human beings, then that sympathy will make you more responsive to them, which will, in turn, make them more responsive to you. To encourage this understanding, we give you the inside goods on the often distorted view from the professor's side of the podium, and we show you how to use the foibles and idiosyncracies of your professors, as well as the weaknesses of the university system, to the advantage of your transcript.

Professors are generally not well-socialized animals. Think about it; they entered college in their late teens and never left. They've lived exclusively in libraries and cafeterias, and the highlight of their professional lives is the academic conference, where they read aloud to seven or eight assembled nerds in clothes that would make even golfers and grandparents giggle. To make matters worse, the very nature of their profession ensures that they are constantly reminded of their fading vigor. Their students enjoy a seemingly perpetual youth; on the exit of each graduating class enters a new crop of nubile bodies. And the professor just keeps getting older and more removed. But the average student understands none of this. Nor do students know the extent to which awareness of this kind of thing can be played to get better grades out of this strange animal. Using caricatures, anecdotes, and situations hypothetical and all too real, *The Savvy Student* will show you how to negotiate the political minefield of college and university education.

Knowing the way your professor sees such things as essay papers, tests, examinations, phone calls, office visits, lecture hours, and any of the other kinds of contact with students will help you understand how best to behave in these situations so that the professor will carry away from his contact with you a positive impression. It is this positive impression that he will bring to his grading of your assignments, and that will make it difficult for him to give you grades that he knows will make you unhappy with him or grades that might compromise your future.

Our book explodes the myth that the grading process is in any way objective, and reveals how and why the grade you receive depends not only on the person doing the grading but also on her impression of you—not your work, *you*! If the professor thinks you're a jerk, the professor will prove this to herself through evaluation of your work; if the professor thinks that you're committed to and engaged in the course (and, better still, that you admire her in some way), then the professor, never one to be wrong in judgment, will find support for these perceptions of you in your work.

If you can master the subjective aspect of grading, that gray zone of the grade that depends on events seemingly outside the work itself, and if you can get yourself into the small inner circle of those students who are familiar, sympathetic, and comforting to the professor, you will turn your 88 into a 90 (and, hence, your B into an A). And, in a school where the transcripts use grade points rather than percentages, this difference of 2 or 3 percent can translate into the difference between a 3.5 and a perfect score of 4.0. Your mastery will also mean that you will have made a powerful ally in the university system who has a stake in your future—not only will your professor reward you with better grades but he will become your reliable source for letters of recommendation praising your abilities, letters that will be crucial for your future in other programs or professions. Membership has its advantages.

So how do you get into the inner circle of privilege? And if you make it in, how do you stay in this position, which is both profitable and perilous? *The Savvy Student* shows you how to be artful without revealing your artifice. It teaches you that all moments of contact should be thought of as performances and that you have to be conscious of the impression you are creating (because you can be damn sure the professor is filing it away for future reference).

The two primary zones of contact between you and your professor are the classroom and the office, and *The Savvy Student* scrutinizes the dynamics of both arenas. Differentiating between the professor's inner circle of students and those students who are wallpaper, this book provides the blueprint of the political architecture of the classroom: we'll tell you where to sit and why; how to ask and how to answer a question in a way that creates a beneficial impression; and how to provide the kinds of verbal and visual feedback to professors that will make them invest themselves in your success. From the dynamics of the office visit to writing a personal message on the final examination paper, *The Savvy Student* probes academic life, reveals its politically charged atmosphere, and lets you know how to be puppet masters and to pull the right strings.

So who the hell are we to tell you this? Well, we're both professors in our early thirties, old enough to know the game well, yet not so old that we've forgotten what it is like to be on your side of the podium. We also share 15 years' teaching experience at several universities (and if you throw in our time as students, graduate students and teaching assistants, we're talking way too many years to admit to in print). So we've both encountered a wide variety of students and behaviors; we've seen successful strategies, and we've witnessed and been on the receiving end of thousands of awkward, skittish and gangly moments of contact that only ended up harming the student in the long run (and in the transcript). We have also listened carefully over many years, and over many beers, to the stories of our war-weary colleagues, stories retold for you here like case studies in what to do and what not to do. Finally, we both managed to emerge from the system with Ph.D.s, so, while we may have received lousy career counseling ourselves, you can at least be sure we learned a thing or two about manipulating our own professors—and we pass our savings on to you!

The Savvy Student probes with humor the psychology of the person students have to deal with every day of their university career, the professor. It is, at times, cynical, certainly provocative, perhaps even controversial, and, oh yes, practical. It provides you with a view from the inside that will give you insight and power, the power to make your transcript more attractive to graduate and professional schools without the sweat of working harder or the inky mess of tampering documents.

So take out your highlighter or a sharp pencil because there's going to be a test. Turn over the page and begin with our diagnostic, a quiz that playfully raises the situational issues of professor-student encounters—those moments when you are, whether you know it or not, making "the grade."

CHAPTER 1

✻ ✻ ✻

Pop Quiz

ARE YOU AN ANNOYING STUDENT?

(Circle the answers that would most likely apply to your responses to the given questions. If you begin to panic, fall asleep, "rebel against the system," or foam at the mouth halfway through the quiz, then turn quickly to Chapter 2—you need this book most of all.)

1. **Your professor has misspelled a word on the blackboard. You would—**
   A say nothing—not now or ever.
   B put up your hand and, when acknowledged, ask politely whether or not the word is spelled correctly.
   C draw attention loudly to the error and tell the professor that you will be deducting 10 percent from his teaching evaluation for sloppiness.
   D walk to the board in exaggerated steps (shaking your head in disgust), take the eraser from the professor's hand, and correct the mistake in two-foot-high block letters.
   F elbow your neighbor and, continuously sniggering, shout, "Duh, better call Vanna. Looks like it's time to buy a vowel!"

2. **Each time that you make a point in class, your professor—**
   A says that you have just touched on a completely original

6

point and instructs the class to write down in their notes what you have just said.

ß   agrees, says that you have made a good point, and moves on.

C   acknowledges your comment with a hand gesture and changes the topic.

D   giggles uncontrollably, asking several times if you are "for real."

F   stares blankly at you for four or five minutes, takes a deep breath, and dismisses the class for the day.

3.   **If you saw your professor out shopping for a light fixture in a hardware store, you would probably be inclined to—**

A   approach, converse politely for a minute, and, when leaving, tell her it was nice to see her.

ß   approach, attempt a joke about how you would have expected that her brilliant thoughts would turn on the lights in her house, and leave.

C   not approach at all, even if she has seen and recognized you.

D   approach, make the same joke as in option "b," but then hang around for a long time, waiting for the big laugh and repeating the words, "D'you get it? No, really, d'you get it?"

F   not be able to decide whether to approach or not, and subsequently follow her around the store for a half hour, grunting aloud your feelings of self-loathing.

4.   **When another student in class is obviously annoying the professor with disrespectful behavior, you would be inclined to—**

A   sit as far as possible from that student, in an effort to dissociate yourself from the annoyance in your professor's mind.

ß   find a way to communicate to the professor (through, say, conspiratorial eye rolling) that you are as annoyed with this behavior as he is.

C   do nothing at all out of the ordinary.

D   take notes each time the student gets off a "good one" against the professor, and, at the end of the year, ask the professor if you will be responsible for memorizing that student's insults for the final exam.

F   befriend the offensive student, whispering an encouraging, "Right on, way to stick it to the man" after each particularly irksome statement.

5. **If you arrive to class late, your normal reaction would be to—**

A   grin apologetically at the professor and take your seat as quietly as possible.

B   do anything that you can to avoid meeting the professor's eyes before you are comfortably settled into your position.

C   stop the class by whispering to the professor that you are late for a good reason, which you will explain later.

D   stop the class by announcing that you are late because you were at wart removal therapy and ask if you have missed anything important.

F   give all your friends "high fives" on your way to your seat, and ask them if "old numb nuts" has said anything useful yet.

6. **If your professor catches you not paying attention and asks you a question that you obviously cannot answer, you would probably—**

A   realize that you have been caught, and lighten the atmosphere by making a joke about being really out of it that day.

B   just admit that you don't know the answer and hope that the professor lets you off the hook by moving on.

C   first try to fake it and then, realizing that you are not going to get away with it, resort to making a joke about not having paid enough attention.

D   try to fake it, and even when it becomes evident to everyone that you have no idea what you are talking about, you would not back down, but rather pretend that you are simply interpreting the material at a level higher than that of the professor and your classmates.

F   become hostile, challenging the professor with taunts like, "Why're ya asking *me*, huh big shot? Ain't it your job to know the answers to these questions, huh big man?"

7. **If your professor goes from person to person, asking students what they expect from the course, you would probably respond with—**

A   "I want to expand my knowledge of the topic, and I've heard good things about the class from former students."

B   "I know a lot about fields related to this subject, so I thought I should probably round out my knowledge."

C   "Well, my friend Shirley took your course last year and really liked it. And, like, she got an A, so . . ."

D   "I expect to get an A so that eventually I can get into law school and take over my father's lucrative practice. What course is this anyway?"

F   "I expect an easy ride; I heard the course was a 'bird,' and I'm hopping on the bandwagon, man."

8. **If you were going to write a short farewell message to your professor at the end of an exam paper, it might read something like—**

A   Thanks for the course. It was great. Have a good summer.

B   Fun course. All the best.

C   Please excuse my handwriting. I get cramps.

D   I could have written more, but my inner child wants to go play on the swings in the park. I can supply a note from my analyst, if necessary.

F   I could have said more, but I had to leave the exam early to catch my plane to Hawaii. Have a good Christmas here in town.

9. **If you have your hand up in class to ask a question or to comment on the material, and the professor is obviously ignoring your hand, you will normally—**

A   recognize that the professor does not want to lose momentum, and lower your hand, trusting that you will be remembered and called upon soon.

ß   lower your hand temporarily, but continue to raise it as a reminder each time there is a natural break in the flow of the lecture.

C   not only keep your hand up continuously but support it with your other hand and grunt a few times to suggest the physical strain of the wait.

D   begin speaking, uninvitedly, shouting louder and louder in an effort to drown out "that ol' blow horn behind the podium."

F   fake an epileptic seizure, and when the paramedics arrive and begin to carry you out on the stretcher, sit up and begin, "Good, now that I have your attention, can you clarify that point about Marx's dialectic?"

10. If you ask a question in class that the professor is obviously having trouble answering, you would probably—

A   seize the opportunity to ingratiate yourself by letting the professor off the hook and ask if he would rather you come back to that point next class.

ß   suggest that it was a stupid question anyway and that his inability to answer it only proves his superior intellect.

C   do nothing, allowing the professor to squirm in the effort to string a few words together.

D   repeat, every minute or so, as you are watching the professor struggle to answer your question, "Well? Huh? C'mon . . . at least take a shot."

F   take out your "Stump the Prof" Tote Board, and slowly begin scribbling your name, the professor's name, the date, and the wording of your question.

11. If you want an extension on your essay, chances are that you will—

A   approach the professor well in advance of the due date, offering an excuse and/or the proper documentation, if necessary.

ß   tell the professor a few days before the due date that you have four other essays due that week and allow him to offer you an extension.

C approach the professor the day that the essay is due, claiming that you have tried your best and that you hope your grade won't be jeopardized if you get it in as soon as possible.

D just hand it in late, and, if a late penalty is enforced, say, "Wow, man, are you an anal-retentive fascist or what?"

F not bother handing in the essay at all, and when the professor shows you, on the course outline, where it says that you will fail if you do not complete the assignment, ask (with genuine disbelief), "You mean you were serious about that?"

12. **If the essay you were sure was worth an A is handed back to you with a 78, you would—**

A take the essay home, read all the comments carefully, and think about your response to them. Then you would arrange an office visit, go over the paper with the professor, pointing to specific areas at issue, explain how much work went into the assignment, and ask that it be given another reading.

B arrange an office visit during which you will explain that such a grade might jeopardize your standing in your program or your chances for a scholarship.

C take the essay home, read all the comments, and, beside each, construct a careful rebuttal. You would then give the annotated paper back to your professor for reconsideration.

D tell the professor that all of your other professors give you higher grades (whether it is true or not) and suggest that there must be something wrong with this professor if she alone has failed to recognize your true genius.

F tear the essay into strips and force-feed it to your professor's cat.

13. **If, during the break in the middle of the class, the professor holds out a dollar bill and aks if anyone is going over to pick up coffee at the cafeteria, you might—**

A offer to pick up coffee for him, whether you were originally planning to go or not (refusing even to think of taking his dollar).

B do the same as option "A" except that you take the dollar.

C do the same as option "B" except you remind him that a coffee actually costs $1.10 and stand waiting for him to fish out the additional dime.

D do the same as option "C" except that you ask to borrow an additional $1.10 so that you can get yourself a coffee too.

F not offer to pick up a coffee for him, deciding instead to lecture him for ten minutes on the negative effects of coffee on his health.

14. **If, during a visit to the professor's office, you notice that she has displayed a photo of her children, you might—**

A say that the children are lovely and then quickly proceed to another topic.

B ask how the professor manages both a busy professional schedule and parenting duties.

C say nothing even though the professor has noticed you looking at the photo and seems to be waiting expectantly for some compliment.

D ask if they were "fun" to conceive.

F mention that you will probably never have children because you have never managed to attract a boyfriend or girlfriend, and ask if you might stop by the professor's place once in a while to play.

15. **If you have not said anything in class all semester because you are by nature a shy person, and you are desperate to make yourself noticed in the final few weeks, you might be inclined to—**

A ask a couple of intelligent questions that you have formulated from your readings prior to class.

B offer to read from the course material when the professor asks for volunteers in class.

C conspicuously move your chair to the front of the room and nod your head in agreement at everything the profes-

sor says, including "Stop nodding your head, you're driving me crazy!"

D put up your hand after each major section and repeat back
the information the professor has just finished outlining,
beginning each time with the statement, "So you mean
that . . ."

F stop wearing pants.

**16. If your professor failed to show up for a scheduled appoint-
ment or office hour, you would—**

A wait until the following day, tell the professor that you
understand her action as a normal mistake, and ask if you
might reschedule.

B leave a note on the door suggesting strongly that you feel
it is now the professor's obligation to contact you to reschedule the appointment.

C call the professor at home, remind her of the appointment,
and ask if you can talk instead over the phone at that
moment.

D decide to wait sitting on the floor outside the professor's
office for the professor to remember the appointment, even
if it takes a week.

F use this mistake at every opportunity to bring the professor "down a peg," including making the quotes sign in
the air with your fingers each time you say the phrase
"office hours."

**17. If you missed several classes in a row, you would probably
consider it a good idea to—**

A approach the podium at the end of the first class you return to and briefly apologize for your absences (being careful to attend each class after that—but not making any
promises).

B get the notes and say nothing about it.

C drop the course and avoid the professor until graduation.

D make the first paragraph on your next assignment an account of your problems, tying them gracefully into the
topic of the essay.

F give the professor the name and number of a proctologist and say that the doctor will explain in detail exactly why you had to be away so long.

18. Your professor's fly is open. You—
A do absolutely nothing—you can't win this one.
B use a form of sign language borrowed from interpretive dance to try to signal the professor.
C giggle uncontrollably and, when asked, refuse to say why.
D undo your own fly as a show of solidarity.
F put up your hand and, when acknowledged, say something cryptic like, "I see it's open season for hunting snakes."

19. You run into your professor at a movie. You—
A leave her to enjoy the movie and next class casually ask her what she thought of the film.
B say "hi" if you make eye contact, and get the hell out of the theater as soon as the credits roll.
C yell "hey" across the theater and, when she turns around, ask if this'll be on the final.
D go to her row and ask, "Mind if I join you?"
F be very quiet and when the lights go down begin a measured but relentless attack with jujubes.

20. It's 2:15 p.m. and your professor's office hours are 1:00 to 2:00 p.m. You go by his office and the door is open. You—
A knock softly, apologize for being late, and ask if it would be okay to ask a brief question.
B go down the hall to the pay phone, call the professor's office, tell him you're on campus, and ask if he has some time.
C listen outside his door for a break in the argument he is having on the phone, pop your head in, and ask, "Hey there, got a minute?"
D go down the hall to the pay phone, call the professor's office, and ask if his refrigerator's running.
F wait silently around the corner, and when he leaves his

office, follow him into the washroom and ask your question over the stall door.

Bonus Question
21. You're driving home through the rain, and you see your professor standing by her broken-down car. You—
A   stop and offer a ride.
B   duck down as you drive by.
C   stop beside her and say, "You see, that's what you get."
D   stop and offer a ride, later asking for gas money.
F   aim for a puddle and send up an arc of water that plasters her to the side of her car.

SCORING

Award yourself 5 points for each "A" answer, 4 points for each "B" answer, 3 points for each "C" answer, 2 points for each "D" answer, and 0 for each F answer. (If you are incapable of doing the math, you might as well just give yourself 0 for everything.) Total your score and find what range you fit in below.

85 TO 105

You are obviously one of those students at the front of the class— with the clean, pressed shirt and the perfect part down the center of your hair—and since your first day of kindergarten you've been responding to every question thrown at you with the kind of wit and flair that makes the professor love you (or at least you think they do), your parents boast about you to the chagrin of all their friends, and the other students want to insert daggers between your shoulder blades. You are very sympathetic toward the precarious position of the professor and have great common sense about how to leave the best impression. The thing is, if you are doing all of this, you might be overplaying your hand. You need to think carefully about subtlety and sincerity. Don't forget, your profs were students once, too—so they can recognize (and despise) an ass kisser when they see one. So read on.

50 TO 84

If you're in this category, you're probably among the multitudes who have arrived in college after years of terrorizing your high school teachers; you sense that your professors deserve a small measure of respect, but you're not sure why—and you certainly have no idea how to give it to them. Your instincts aren't bad, but you haven't clearly figured out the dynamic of professor-student relationships. You're in grave danger of making very costly mistakes. Read on.

0 TO 49

This is a failing grade. My God, you're in desperate shape. We can picture you now—snoozing at the back of our classrooms—telling all your friends that "it's okay because Woody Allen got thrown out of college in his day, too," trying to convince your parents that your grades would be better except that "nobody understands you." Continue on this path and you'll find your picture pasted on "Most Unwanted" signs in every faculty lounge in the country, followed, of course, by a rewarding career asking future business customers if they would "like fries with that?" Please, please, read on.

CHAPTER 2

* * *

I Gotta Be Me

THE SUBJECTIVE ASPECT OF GRADING

FAIR PLAY

At a hockey tournament last winter to watch a talented friend play, we were struck by a strange phenomenon. This tournament was the last major event before the draft, so everybody's nerves were doing caffeine back-flips. Sitting in the stands among his relatives, we watched penalty after penalty get called against our team. It came to the point where, each time the whistle blew, our little pocket of spectators would react as hired mourners would at the funeral of some national leader. Our reactions suggested something about what we expected from the referees. We looked to them for impartiality. Those special uniforms were supposed to mean something. To the scouts in attendance, there was nothing unusual about local referees favoring the local team or this favoritism influencing their evaluation of the team's performance (to the disadvantage of the competition). And if you talk to referees, they'll tell you that, even during the course of a game, they form opinions about players ("this one looks like a bruiser"; "this one's good"; "this one plays rough"; "I gotta watch this one for holding.") Those judgments influence what the referees see out on the ice. Unfair as it may seem, most of the time, these opinions are formed on the basis of only the first few minutes of play.

Well, we're not referees, but we're here to tell you the same human frailty exists among your professors. The university classroom is not a hockey rink, but it can be just as slippery, and, though they don't wear the black-and-white stripes, your professors are calling the game and its outcome will have a lot to do with their own biases and personal quirks. The outcome will also play a large role in your future success.

BEING SUBJECTED TO THE SUBJECTIVE

The notion of objectivity has taken a beating lately. Just look at the study of history: once regarded as the objective recording of past events as fact, it has now been argued to be almost the same as fiction, in that it too is told by a biased narrator who influences the way in which events are told. Take Christopher Columbus for instance: Italian hero and revolutionary European geographer, or a native-whomping pirate with a thirst for Isabella's jewels? Depends who's writing the history you're reading. And when it comes to grading assignments, the same principle applies. There is no objective position. The grade you receive will always be dependent on who's doing the grading and on that person's impression of you (not your work, *you!*).

Put yourself in our out-of-fashion shoes for a minute: it's late one evening during the midwinter break, and you're snowed under by a pile of essays so high that frost is forming on its upper pages. In the apartment below, your neighbors are drinking well-rummed eggnog and being noisily festive. Hell, you may be a professor, but even you are entitled to a little celebration—if only you didn't have to face these essays. Then you come to an essay written by a guy who has spent the entire term sleeping off his drunken binges in the desk two rows to the left of your podium (that is, on the rare occasion when he bothers to show up to your class at all). Are you going to be resentful? What's going through your mind as you read the first of 11 pages? Well, first of all, you're probably imagining him as one of the egg-nogged revelers in the apartment below. Then you start thinking: "I'm gonna have to spend 45 minutes to an hour on this guy, who's likely under a table somewhere in Florida, tanned, laughing, surrounded by other beautiful bodies, and who doesn't give a damn what I think." And then you come across a simple mistake (in spelling or form or accuracy) and BOOM! this essay gets nailed. You're thinking: "If this guy had been listening he never would have done this" or "I corrected this error twice on his last paper; he's obviously not reading my comments, so to hell with him!" The party downstairs gets louder, and each page seems to take longer to get through on your way to the last. When you do get there, all the resentment that has built up on your way through the paper gets dumped into a number that is as low as you believe you can defend (lower, even, than how you feel at that moment). You may even think, consciously, that you are being fair, but, subconsciously, something else is at work. You're punishing. You're exercising the only power you've got, and you're working out the frustration you feel. Welcome to the professoriate!

Or, perhaps this happens. It's late one evening during the midwinter break, and you're snowed under by a pile of essays so high that frost is forming on its upper pages. In the apartment below, your neighbors are drinking well-rummed eggnog and being noisily festive. Then you come to an essay written by a student who has been a pleasure to work with all term (in other words, she has carefully executed all the advice in this book). She has attended class regularly. She has paid attention and participated. She has come to your office a few times to ask some well-thought-out questions about the preparation of her essay. This time, when you hit a spelling error or grammatical problem, it doesn't mean as much; this time, instead of looking for ways to penalize the student, you're actively looking for the strengths to reward. Don't get us wrong, you'd still rather be doing something else, but this student has given you reason to be sympathetic to her, and you meet her paper with all the holiday spirit you can muster. The truth of the matter is, this student is no smarter than the one in the previous example—this student probably hasn't even worked harder on her paper than the other student. All that matters is that this student has played the game better. This student has worked you that much better and has ended up with a grade that reflects intelligence and effort, whether or not she possesses that intelligence or has truly made the effort.

With the possible exception of the multiple choice examination, every grade you receive is, to some extent, subjective; that is, the grade you receive is at least partially dependent on the response to you of the person doing the grading. This is true of everything from short-answer questions through to the longer essay, from chemistry problems to lab reports. Wherever it is possible to evaluate a degree of accuracy, wherever one final number or one precise term does not constitute the entire grade, and wherever your professor has to grade your approach to a problem in addition to your final answer, you are playing in the realm of a professor's subjective judgment. (If this wasn't the case, we would never have passed calculus.)

The smallest details will matter in all instances. Let's say that you are taking a film quiz, and the professor asks, "Who directed *Taxi Driver*?" You know the answer, but you forget the spelling, so you scribble "Skoresayzee." Now, if you have not shown interest in the class all year, if you've missed half the lectures and passed notes to your friends throughout the other half, then you're getting the goose egg for that answer. If, however, you have attended class and participated so that the professor will remember hearing you say "Scorsese" properly on many occasions, you'll get the grade. This will happen hundreds of times during your university career on assignments worth anywhere from 1 to 100 percent of your final grade, and you have to know the tricks to tip the scales in your favor every time.

There are many things over which you have no control, but doing those things within your power can give you a certain influence over the moment when that magic (and usually random) number is pulled from your professor's hat.

''I SEE,'' SAID THE BLIND MAN

In an attempt to overcome some of the subjective aspects of grading, some professors practice something called "blind grading." This means that they obscure or intentionally ignore the name of the student on the paper so that, ideally, their personal feelings about their students cannot influence the grade. (Of course, the fact that this grading technique even exists only proves how subjective our responses to students and the grading process really are.) Ultimately this practice, in theory, can help produce a more objective evaluation of the individual assignment, but somewhere along the way professors are going to have to put a number beside your name, and they know they have final control over that number. If they want to doctor the figures, there is no IRS to call them in for an audit; they'll find a way to give you a number that they are happy with. So that even if professors grade all assignments blindly, they will end up with, say, five students at the end of the year with a grade of 88 percent. The two students who have played the game well and made a positive impression will automatically be bounced up a notch to the elusive 90 percent level, and those two extra points will put them in a much better position when it comes to applying for graduate or professional school. The two neutral students will stay at 88 percent, while the grade of the one annoying student will find itself spiraling in a free fall. This is where the notion of creative math comes into play.

DAVID: I tried blind grading myself one year, and I found that, with the majority of my students, it worked: a student's grade could go up or down, and I recorded the grade as I scored it on the individual paper or exam. But there was this inner circle in each of my classes that I could not be blind to. First of all, I could usually spot the writing styles of the people in this small group (in fact, it became a kind of game to me): ''This sounds like something Samantha would say'' or ''He's using the same terms we talked about when he came to see me in my office.'' This recognition immediately brought the person to the table, and objectivity went out the window.

Usually this works in the student's favor because we, as professors, tend to be able to recognize more readily the work of students we like. So when it comes to assigning the grade, that positive attitude toward the student bumps the grade a shade higher. (And dammit, who can resist the temptation to fold back the page to reveal the name of the student before the grading is done anyway?) What we're telling you with all this is that it is to your advantage to become one of the inner circle of students that the professor will recognize and try to reward.

OUT OF CONTROL

Quite a number of things you might not expect figure into your grade, and many of these things are completely beyond your control. Professors are not computers; they have good days and bad days, good moments and bad moments. If they sit down to grade your essay, and they've just had an argument with the chair of their department over a promotion or their allowance of photocopies, they can't help but bring that to their desks with them. Something as arbitrary as where your paper falls in the pile also contributes to your grade. If yours is the last essay before bed, it gets attention that is a little less focused (the professor is already seeing freedom and escape). This usually translates into a higher grade for the paper under consideration—the professor feels a little guilty about her distracted reading (she can't quite remember what it was you wrote on pages 3 through 5), though she's not feeling so guilty that she'll read the thing again. But, if yours is the third essay of three bad essays in a row, then, man, are you in for it. Your paper will bear the weight of that accumulated disgust and anger. The professor will feel her time has been wasted and hold you largely responsible—every small error that resembles the errors of the other papers becomes a big, big error. We know it's not fair, but it's true. Professors are like anybody else; they can't just turn off the world and encounter your work unencumbered. They take everything with them to your essay—their fight with their spouse, their car that won't start, their house-plants dying. And you may be the victim.

The words of another professor can also be influential in determining your grade. You should know that professors talk to one another about students (there's no confidentiality of the confessional here). Younger professors tend to be even more dangerous in this regard (and this is only because generally the older ones have stopped talking to each other altogether). Many is the time we've listened to (okay, and participated in) the bar-room discussion of a particular "problem" student who a few of us have in common. This seemingly idle chit-chat can work against you. A close acquaintance tells the story of getting slotted as a B student by one professor, and this particular professor's gossipy nature infected her relationship with other professors. Professor X was in Professor Y's office discussing the weather, when all of a sudden her name comes up. Professor X, who has seen one paper, tells

Professor Y that she's a B student. Later that month Professor Y sits down to grade our friend's work; that conversation echoes in the mind of Professor Y, and guess what letter he comes up with? (She had received only A's in college to that point, but one nonbeliever had, overnight, begun an epidemic of B's.) So don't be fooled; peer pressure doesn't stop when you get out of high school—professors feel it too.

On the flip side, if you are aware of this gossipy tendency, you can use it to your advantage. For, in addition to many sessions of tearing students to shreds, we have also participated in great defense of students we thought well of. One particular student we knew, was, by the time she graduated, well on her way to having her own fan club established among the faculty—we still talk about how much we miss her. Okay, she may have been genuinely intelligent, but there are a few bright lights in every classroom; something else set her apart. She was always visibly engaged by the material under consideration. If she didn't like or understand a particular work or section, she would try to analyze that problem and come away from the material with whatever she could. She accepted the weaknesses and limitations of her professors but, instead of exposing those weaknesses, she set out to take from those professors the best they had to offer. It was this constant good intention toward her work and her professors that got people talking about her. And this paid off big time. She pulled very high numbers, and, though her work was strong, the numbers were not entirely due to this strength; the grades she received also had much to do with our sense of her as we sat down to evaluate her work. (In other words, an A was translated into an A+, that A+ was translated into law school, law school was translated into big bucks—you know the rest.)

THAT'S PROGRESS

Another aspect of the problem of subjectivity in grading is that professors frequently believe in progress. Professors rarely treat your individual assignments as isolated events in themselves. Each assignment will almost always be seen in relation to your previous work. And some professors will mentally, perhaps subconsciously, chart a trajectory through a course that might very well depend exclusively on the grade they give the first piece of work you submit. They'll take that 73 you got on the first assignment and lock you into a nice slow gradation upward, over the course of, say, four assignments, and you might finish the year breaking into the B range (too late, of course, to outweigh the bulk of your year, so you average out safely in mid-C land). If you score an 81 on the first assignment, then when he comes to the second assignment, sometimes with his grade sheet open beside him, he's thinking, "Okay, an 84 or a 78 is reasonable—this student will probably land in this range." And sure enough, the prophet fulfills his own predictions, and you land within the professor's little comfort zone. If, when he comes to enter the result on the grade sheet, the new grade seems out of whack with the previous ones, he'll second-guess himself, return for a quick scan, and probably adjust the grade up or down (usually this process is employed to lower grades rather than raise them). Some professors will intentionally lowball you on the first assignment just to allow themselves room to give you a slowly measured increase through the course of the year (you end up feeling as though you are improving, and they end up looking as though they helped you improve). So remember, assignments don't exist in vacuums; don't wait until the end of the year to pull out all the stops—by then it may be too late for recovery. And by all means, if you find yourself slotted in a low range after your first assignment, then you must find a way, skillfully, gracefully, to elevate your standing—to make the professor think that he may actually have been wrong about you when he gave you that first grade.

PICKING AND CHOOSING

Let's face it, some professors are just plain jerks about grades. (For a comprehensive list, please send $800 and a self-addressed stamped envelope to . . . Nah, better not. We're in enough trouble as it is.) It is not unusual to come across professors who don't believe in grades over 85. For them, grades over 90 are reserved for some rarefied ideal performance of which even they can't quite conceive. You see, to give you such a grade would be to compromise their own hold on the intellectual property; they'd have to admit that you know the stuff—that they are not the only ones capable of understanding such advanced, subtle material. And many professors are not that strong. They want to make sure that the movement of information occurs from the top down and that they stay firmly at the top.

Some professors are simply spiteful and will act unpredictably, usually hurting students who have good records up until that point. You don't have to be an A student to feel the sting of these ones: everyone in the class is, before the paper is even written, disadvantaged with them because their ceiling is lower, and so all grades will be correspondingly lower. If at all possible, avoid these professors. If you're a first-year student, then you're going to have trouble finding out who they are and even more trouble arranging your courses to avoid them—but you should work extra hard to look for subtle clues from upper-level students in your residences, at early school functions, or simply through the rumor mill.

For those of you in upper years, keep your ears open and register early to avoid the embittered jerks who seem to exist only to destroy students' self-esteem. But, with shrinking departmental budgets and increasing class sizes (and, for professors, increasing course loads), getting your choice of professors is going to be more and more difficult. So you're going to have to develop survival strategies. With these professors especially, but actually with all professors, there are ways to help your cause and ways to play the game so that you can have at least some control over how they perceive you and what grade they are going to place next to your name. Even with an odd professor, you can put the odds in your favor.

The most important thing within your control is your personal presence in the professor's mind when she sits down to grade your work. The professor comes to your work with preconceived notions of what it might be like. If she thinks you're a slacker who doesn't really get it, then she's only going to try to prove herself right when she comes to your paper—she'll look for those moments that reinforce her opinions of you. On the other hand, if the professor has been led to believe that you are an interested and thoughtful student, then she'll find in your work a reflection of that opinion that you have strived to create.

NUDGE NUDGE, WINK WINK

We've had students in our courses finish with a numerical grade of 69—but giving them this grade would be like begging them to launch an appeal. The appeal is the bane of the professor's existence; it means rereading all assignments, meetings with various administrative people, and plenty of paper shuffling. We've got better things to do, especially when we had put that class to bed in our minds and moved onto bigger and better things. There is also an element of pride that comes into play: suddenly, the professor is put in the position where he has to defend his ability to judge the student—the thin facade of authority is in danger of being torn down. Because of these potential hassles, professors will look for ways to avoid the appeal. The most typical way is the grade nudge. If a student's grade mathematically calculates in at a "9" station (59, 69, 79), then we take it up a notch or down a notch. A 68 or a 70, for instance, is much less likely to be protested than a 69 because the 68 is far enough away from the border to the next level, and the 70, though just barely, has made it.

Now, whether that grade nudge takes you a notch up or a notch down will depend entirely on the nature of the relationship you establish with your professor over the course of the year.

UNDER PRESSURE

Now that we have established that there is no such thing as objectivity in grading, or in your professor's approach to your performance in a course, it might be worthwhile to examine the various factors that go into the process of coming up with your grades. You should remember that your professor does not exist in a vacuum (though it might be tempting to throw him in one and watch the result). He is part of a large institution which is constantly placing demands upon him, and these demands may or may not conform to how he sees the system in its ideal form. The process of grading is like a tightrope walk; professors have to please themselves, their university, and the students all at the same time, and these three forces very rarely agree. Professors are constantly looking for ways to compromise that allow them to get through the process in a way that will satisfy everyone, and you have to understand these compromises to exploit them.

Perhaps the first and most important aspect of the professor's approach to assigning grades is the fact that, upon entering the classroom, she already has some vague idea both of what the average mark in the class is going to be and of the scale into which all the grades in the class will fit. What this means is that before your professor even meets you and your classmates, she has decided the class average will be, say, somewhere around 75 percent. (There is nothing more agonizing for a professor than ending up with a class full of Einsteins and looking for ways to find fault in the most gifted students because the university would not tolerate too many high grades.) Also, in order to achieve this average of 75 percent, she will not give half the class grades in the 90s, and the other half grades in the 40s. Nor will she imagine that she can get away with giving everyone in the class a 75, unless she's committed to old-style communism, where everyone is believed to be equal. Although each professor takes a different approach to this ideal average and to this scale, most will understand that if there are fifty people in the class, there will be about ten A's, maybe twenty B's, and twenty C's and D's combined, with a few (maybe three in each category) stragglers who will defy the odds and reach the A+ level or the F level.

Why are these scales and these averages necessary? The answer is the most basic and common response possible—FEAR. And what do professors fear most? They fear the kind of trouble that will disrupt their normal, calm, contemplative life. Professors have it pretty good—they can't be fired, they earn a decent living, they avoid many of the vulgarities of the real world in their little privileged tower, and they really aren't looking for a fight. They fear being the one to rock the boat, and they fear having to answer for their grades. They are survival oriented and they know that, in order to survive in their department, their grades must fit a particular scheme that has, on some implicit (sometimes explicit) level, been agreed upon by the entire department. If one professor was consistently to give all A's or all F's, then the department would be thrown out of balance, and students would give the department hassles because of correctly perceived inconsistencies within various courses. There is a story of one clever part-time professor who, when he found out the department had not renewed his contract for the following year, gave all his students

F's so that the department would have the headache of a full summer of appeals. He would have been wiser to give all A's, since that would have really disrupted the system throughout the entire department. Instead of pissing off his students, he would have pissed off every other student in the school, as well as all his colleagues, who would have looked like jerks in the process.

Don't forget that universities are businesses, and individual departments are businesses too; if a department gets a bad reputation among students, then that business would quickly find itself in a great deal of trouble, financial and otherwise. It is also true that universities see grades as meaning something. If a school wants to prove that it has higher standards than its main rival, it will probably pride itself on giving lower grades. These grades are interpreted as meaning that the education at one school is better than the next, that their courses are more meaningful. It is a false way of constructing the meaning of a grade, but it happens all the time. The same will happen with individual professors who will give lower grades just to prove that their standards are higher and their lectures more intense, even though the material is exactly the same as in every other section of the course.

There are two things that students can learn from this awareness of the department as business: first, departments must do what they have to do (particularly with regard to grades) to keep attracting students, and second, students ultimately have a lot more power in the system than they might realize.

By writing that professors are made to understand that their grades must fit a certain scheme, we do not mean to suggest that professors attend meetings in which they are told that their average grade must be, say, 72 percent, and that they must have a certain number of grades at each level. Usually this kind of thing will not happen. A grade level will evolve over many years, and a professor will simply know from experience (or, in the case of younger professors, by asking their colleagues) what is considered "normal" in terms of a proper grade scale for a course. This scale is constantly evolving in the university system. It would be easy to trace trends of grade inflation and deflation over periods of many years in a particular school or department. Just ask your parents or your older siblings (or even your professors, if you want to make them nervous) what would have been considered a "good" grade when they were at university (a grade that would, for example, get them into medical or law school). You would probably find that "good" grades are much higher today than they were "way back then." What this means is that grades that were once considered high (B's, for example) are now considered low, and grades that were once considered very high, like moderate-level A's, are now considered fairly average or only slightly above average. As a result, you are put into a position where you have to work the system harder and harder if you want to push your grades up the A scale in order to distinguish yourself from your fellow students and have a chance at gaining entrance to a postgraduate program.

This has become particularly important because the days when a B.A. or B.S. could actually get you a job out there in the world are long gone. These degrees no longer have any professional value except to prepare you for your next degree, whether that degree is in law or medicine or chartered accountancy or an M.B.A. That is why it is absolutely crucial that you approach your bachelor's degree, from your introductory class to your graduation, as a necessary step upward to the next level, not as an end in itself. If you are not working the system from the first day that your parents drop you off in your dorm room onward, you're dead in the water.

MAKING THE GRADES

You may be wondering whether your professor is aware of this grade "scale" at all, and whether it factors into reaching a decision about your grade. Perhaps you would rather think that education is sacred, that if everyone in your class has earned an A then everyone will get an A, and that, conversely, if everyone deserves a D then that is exactly what the professor will give everyone. Well, forget those ideals. Your professor knows where the grades have to be slotted, even if that knowledge is just a tickle at the back of his brain.

In the not-too-distant past, recent enough for many of your professors to remember, this pressure was much more than just a tickle. One colleague talked to us about actually attending a meeting where "grade corridors" were discussed and agreed upon. The introductory course he was teaching was to have a grade average between 65 and 67. What would happen to professors who failed to turn in such an average for their class? Well, no one did. They avoided the hassles. This same colleague told us that, at his department's first-semester meeting each year, they also agreed on "failure ratios": 16 percent of the class was expected to fail. If, at the end of the year, his final tabulations worked out to about an 8 percent failure rate, he was expected to come up with another 8 percent to fail. After all, the department had a standard to uphold.

Departments today tend to be less overt about grading requirements. But, if you're wondering whether, when a professor's grades are ranging off the chart, that professor will be approached by the administration and reprimanded directly, the answer is yes (it happens all the time). It has happened to us on several occasions:

HARRY: My first experience with this kind of thing was when I was a graduate student hired as a grader and TA, and desperate to do a good job for the professor that I was assisting. I was given a one-hour orientation with all the other teaching assistants, during which we were all given the same essay to grade. After grading the essay, we were all supposed to say aloud the grade that we would have given it if it had been submitted by one of our students, and you better believe that the grades we had come up with were supposed to be exactly the same.

So, at the very moment that careers as a university instructor and grader begin, professors are conditioned to the idea that there is an absolute and particular code that defines grading, and all we knew about that code then was that we were supposed to follow someone else's lead.

I, of course, had no idea what I was doing. When it came my turn to call out the grade that I had given the paper, I proudly announced ''71 percent'' because the three people before me had said ''70 percent,'' ''73 percent,'' and ''70 percent.'' In fact, the number written on the page in front of me was ''81 percent.'' I had been given a crash course, and the only lesson was that my own judgment—as a variation from the consensus—would not be tolerated. It was a potent lesson for me and my

young colleagues, all of us desperate to survive in this new
role of authority that we had suddenly, and seemingly by accident, fallen into.

One colleague tells a slightly different story: "At the beginning
of the year, I made it clear to the professor who I was assisting
that I had never assigned grades before and that I did not know
anything about the expected range. Perhaps the most significant
moment of my career as an instructor came with his answer to
my inquiry. He winked at me, and he said, 'Keep your average
at 70 percent, and you won't have any problems.' I did not know
then exactly what was meant by these 'problems,' but I know,
now, that it has something to do with my security, my ability to
advance in the field, and my ability to earn enough money to be
at least comfortable in life. These obscure 'problems' are understood as a threat to stability in the professorial life. I was taught
that they are to be avoided through compromises and concessions
to the larger system."

Everything that has happened to us since those early days has
been consistent with these experiences. The pressure to conform
to grade curves, to avoid appeals, and to resolve things quietly
and privately without troubling the administration, is reinforced
on a day-to-day basis. Still now, it often happens that we will sit
down to grade a stack of midterm exams, and, if the first couple
of students do well, we'll be pleased, because it seems that our
exam has brought out the best in this bunch. But when the next
two or three students also get A's, we begin to worry that we've
made the exam too easy or that the high grades will throw the
entire system or scheme out of whack. From this point on, you'd
better believe that we're looking for ways to cover our tracks and
for opportunities to bring students' grades down because we remember those promised "problems," that first threat that follows
us always. So how do you think your paper will be received when
it is the tenth one we come to after we've given out eight A's and
a B?

Whether or not your professors were ever warned in a direct
way, they too carry around this fear of the "problems" that might
arise if their grades are different from the pack. What you have
to figure out is how to make sure that you are on the higher side

of the grades they must give. While not becoming an additional problem for the professor, your presence in her mind must be such that there is no way she is going to make you part of the attempt to bring the grades down a touch. If anything, another student's grade might suffer so that she can give you the grade she wants to.

> **DAVID:** One year, I was asked to teach a course that, for genera-tions, has had the reputation of being a ''bird'' course, or, as we used to call it when I was a student, a ''blow-off.'' As a result, I allowed my own idealism, for once, to get the better of me, and I actually gave the students the high grades that they deserved in this painfully easy course. The class average was somewhere near or even above the A level, simply because most students, I felt, had actually done the necessary learn-ing for the course—they had achieved its objectives. After submitting these high and honest grades through the normal channels, I quickly found out where ideals will get you in this business. I promptly received a telephone call from my department chair, under the direction of the dean of the fac-ulty, who told me, in no uncertain terms, that my grades were far too high. There were no questions asked like ''Why do your students deserve such good grades?'' or ''Did you happen to have an exceptional group this time around?'' And I wondered why these grades posed such a threat to the university. Did they threaten the reputation of the university, as though if the grades were too high the school might be perceived as not being serious enough about or rigorous enough in the education it gave? Or did the grades suggest that this one course is too easy, as though students would learn of these grades and think that my course was not a real course. Although it was too late to change the grades for this class, I was made to feel as though I had done a disservice to the department.

Believe it or not, the paranoia about grades can go to ridicu-lous extremes. Sometimes, if we detect that the female students in our classes are doing generally better than the male students, or vice versa, we start to worry that some student or the school itself will notice and complain. If we see that one section of a course is getting higher grades than another of our sections, we worry about repercussions. We wish we could say that these worries are the result of our personal paranoia, but the fact is that they are shared by so many of our colleagues that they must come from some other source.

The law of the grade scheme is a tacit agreement. It is understood that this agreement must continue to exist for the sake of the business of education. No one knows what would happen if the agreement broke down. University teaching is a very comfortable job, and no one wants to find out what might happen if the conditions of that comfort were challenged.

THE PROFESSOR'S INHERITANCE

Aside from the actual pressure from above to fit grades into a scheme, you might wonder if professors talk about these grade expectations among themselves in an unofficial way. The answer, again, is yes. A colleague of ours, whenever she teaches a course for the first or second time, always meets with one of the older professors who has taught the course many times to ask what the average grade in her class should be. After that, she shares the information that she has gathered with the other younger professors, all of whom listen very carefully.

In addition, all of your professors, at some point or another, have found themselves team-teaching a course. Here, final grades are agreed upon together. If professors haven't realized that there is a uniform grade scheme prior to this experience, they will certainly never forget it after they have discovered that their grades do not resemble or match those of the other members of the team, and they are forced to take a crash course in grade conformity.

Finally, if you don't think that professors talk casually together about their overall grades and about the grades of individual students that they have in common, then you know nothing about how limited your professors' lives are, or about how few things that they have to discuss among themselves. Eventually, in the course of these more casual, social conversations, your professors will come to recognize that their grade scheme is either too high or too low.

HARRY: I remember once, in the course of a conversation with several friends and colleagues, discovering that my average grade was almost always higher than the rest. I didn't think that this was much of a problem. I claimed that maybe this was the case because I was lucky enough to have been assigned to teach better students, or because I was just a better professor, so naturally my students performed better. My colleagues were not amused. One professor stepped forward and accused me of not taking the task of teaching seriously enough. This colleague claimed that I should recognize that our discipline was a profound one, and that it was therefore, by definition, inaccessible to certain students. The fact that my average was higher meant that I did not respect the difficulty of my own topic of specialization.

This is how far professors will go to protect their sense of their own importance. This is the intimidation that the individual professor remembers each time he looks at the sheet onto which he is going to copy out his final grades.

Despite the experiences we've just shared, you might still ask: do professors actually have this kind of scheme in mind when they are jotting down grades? The answer, really, is yes and no. In some respects, it is like unmarked speed limits on a road. Drivers know that there are certain speeds at which they can drive without getting into trouble with the law—there's a gray area of permissible flexibility. In most cases professors do have a scheme in mind. Perhaps the professor is not thinking all year long in a conscious way about squeezing grades into a scheme, but when at the end of the year that professor is staring down at the piece of paper onto which the grades will be written, then yes, the professor will be wondering if the grades that are about to be submitted will be appropriate—or, to put it in more basic terms, if those grades will allow the professor to continue along with the quiet, normal, uneventful life that she has been enjoying and hopes to continue to enjoy without any trouble. If your professors know that all of their colleagues who are teaching courses at the same level will end the year with an average grade of somewhere around 73 percent, then your professors will probably, somewhere in their mind, be working toward that number as well. Their motivation for this will not necessarily be the fear of proving themselves different from everyone else, but more the fear of the inconvenience that would come with that difference.

THE STUDENTS' SQUEEZE PLAY

This is where the notion of the students' own power in the system comes into play. Students should be aware that they have a great deal more power in their relationship with their professors than they would normally believe. The main factor motivating professors' perceptions of the grading system is the desire not to do anything that might inconvenience them. Teaching, and especially grading, are secondary in most professors' lives. Their priority might be their research, their leisure, or their desire for peace and quiet, but it is *not* the problem of determining the difference between the significance of a grade of 87 percent and a grade of 90 percent.

If you let your professors know that you are the type of student who is going to fight for the 90 percent over the 87 percent, to the point that they would have to work to prove that you really are an 87 percent, then you can rest assured that you will receive the 90 percent without any trouble at all. You will receive the 90 percent, not because there is an actual difference between 87 and 90 percent, but because your professors are working primarily to avoid trouble. Therefore, as much as they will be looking to avoid conflict with the dean and the chair of their department, they will be trying to stay out of trouble with you as well (especially if they feel that you might complain to the dean or the chair). As we will tell you again and again in this book, the only difference between a student earning 87 percent and one earning 90 percent is the fact that professors know that they are expected by the department to achieve a certain distribution of grades in a class, and therefore your professors will be looking for students to give 87 percent to so they can get away with giving the others 90 percent.

In looking at the class, the professor will have a sense not only of who deserves a good grade, but of who is passive enough to accept the high B or C, and who will demand the A. If you present yourself, throughout your university years, as someone who is perfectly happy with B's, then you can be certain that at the end of your four years your transcript will be full of B's, and you will have a very hard time using that transcript to advance yourself in the world of graduate or professional scholarship. If, on the other hand, you present yourself from the start as someone who is driven and ambitious and expecting an A, your professor will pick up on that and look for ways to give you that A so as to avoid any trouble from you. This is not to suggest that you will be guaranteed an A just because you seem to expect one, but first impressions are potent, and the professor will take that impression into the grading of your work.

ADVANTAGE: STUDENT

The key to getting an advantage over your professor in your power dynamic with him is subtlety. If you come on strong—if you let him know straight out that you will fight hard if you don't get the grade that you want—then you will probably make him defiant, determined to fight back against the pressure that you are obviously applying. How, then, are you to let your professors know that you are the type of student who belongs at the top level of the grading scheme? Some answers to this question will be offered in the following chapters of this book that focus on how to behave in the classroom and on how to approach your professor outside the class. But there are also some simple and immediate answers to consider.

For starters, find subtle ways to let your professor know that you intend to apply for a program that will require you to have high grades, and give her the sense that you are well on your way to having the proper requirements already. She will, in turn, give you serious consideration for one of the ration of A's available to distribute in your class. She will also come to understand that you are goal oriented and that you are giving her the chance to contribute to your advancement toward that goal. Professors live with the hope that one of their students will become a big star—at least, they want to be able to say that they knew you when . . . Your job is to give them the sense that you are actually going places ('cause nobody ever takes *them* anywhere) and that you are offering them this one chance to come on board.

A second good strategy might be to mention, on several occasions, the positive experience that you have had in the class of one of your professor's colleagues (provided that you also got an A in that colleague's class). This requires tremendous tact—you must not let the professor fear that you are drawing a potentially unfavorable comparison between him and his colleague. After you do this, you can be almost certain that your professor will mention you to that colleague at some point in the near future, and will hear from that colleague that you are, indeed, a student who belongs at the A level. Once again, when a professor is coming up with your numbers, one of his primary considerations, even if he wants to go against it, is the relation his grade has with the grades that have already been determined for you by other professors.

If you can succeed in building yourself a reputation around the professors in your department as an A-level student throughout your years of university, then you will almost be assured an A before you step into your upper-year classes—the professors will know before they see the first word that you write that you are supposed to receive an A. Reputation is everything. Once again, subtlety is the key in all this. You must never let anyone know that you are actively working your reputation. It must all appear natural, predestined.

THE POLITICS OF DANCING

If nothing else, this chapter is designed to show you that the notion of the "grade," rather than being an intellectual or academic concept, is really a political concept. When you first submit a term paper or an exam at the university level, you may think that your professor is an authority who, unlike you, can carefully measure each statement in your work and detect the subtle differences between a grade of 77 percent and that of 81 percent. But the truth is that this difference does not really exist at all, and your professors' judgment is only partially based upon the impression of your work. The rest is political; the professor is surrounded by pressures from many different sources that ultimately dictate where your grade will fall within some predetermined scheme. Your idealism about the ivory tower might be the first casualty of a political system of grading that was in place long before you came along and will remain when you are gone. Your professors can only read your work through a thick filter of expectations that have been forced upon them and over which they have little control.

But why do you need to know this? Because understanding the system is the first important step in playing the game. Since it is unlikely that you will change the system during your tenure as a student, understanding it will help you get the most out of it. If this system is forcing your professor to slot you into a certain student category, then understanding this system will help you toward knowing how to get slotted into the best category. You have to develop strategies of placing yourself into the category for the allotted number of A's that your professors are permitted (and forced) to assign in your class. After all, it is this very system, unfortunate as it is, that will ultimately determine your future in scholarship and perhaps in life. But, hey, no pressure or anything.

CHAPTER 3

* * *

Showing Class

CATCHING THE EYE WITHOUT THEM CATCHING ON

For the professor, the classroom population divides into two categories: the inner circle of familiar (and favored) students and the wallpaper. For each course that a professor teaches, she can hold only so many faces and names in her mental file. For most, it breaks down at about 40/60: 40 percent of the students will be recognizable to the professor. She will remember your name, think about you from time to time outside of class, and know something about the way you think, your sense of humor, whatever. The rest of you, nameless, vague, interchangeable faces out there, you're wallpaper, baby, and you need this chapter. In the following pages, we want to describe the classroom experience and the lecture as it is understood by the professor. As always in this book, the professor we describe is a fiction based on experience and odds; you're going to have to do your own critical appraisal of where your own professor fits and what of this will apply to her. The names have been changed to protect the (not so) innocent, but the foundation is as real as the transcript you'll receive on graduation day.

CLASS ACTION

In the courses we have taught, there have always been participation grades (usually amounting to about 10 percent of the final grade). Even those classes that do not have specified participation grades will have room for some kind of discretionary grading on the part of the professor—it is this discretionary aspect that you want to have ultimate control over. Although the grade appears to be in the professor's hands, it is not; your presence in the room, your refusal to be wallpaper, will help determine this grade. Each year, at the end of the course, we pore over class lists assigning grades to each name—some names register, and others give us pause. It often happens that, as we're looking over these lists to assign participation grades, a good 50 percent of the class gets a grade picked out of pretty thin air because we have no idea who *such-and-such a student* is. Oh sure, the name looks familiar, we've seen it on essays and assignments, but there's no face in our minds to attach to it, no real person to contend with, and so it's easy for us to just come up with a number that reflects this person's medio-cre presence in our mind (let's say a 6.5 or 7 out of 10; something high enough that the student won't complain and low enough that he won't be rewarded). Some professors, when they hit a name they don't recognize, will simply look at the student's grades on the other assignments and work out an average number based on that—but this book is about getting your relationship with the professor to the point where such a blasé response to your name will be impossible. We want to tell you how to use your perfor-mance in the classroom to make the professors actually *want* to help you when it comes to grading your work—so that when they come across your name on the list, they actually know you, like you, and want to give you a boost. This chapter will tell you how to stand out from the wallpaper and take your place among the few, the chosen (although the choice will have been yours, it will appear to be the professor's), the inner circle.

Making yourself this kind of familiar presence in the classroom will not only help with discretionary grading but will determine to a large extent how the professor will respond to all of your other work as well. If a professor is predisposed to sympathize with, admire, or like you, then your written work will be destined for a higher grade than it might receive if you fail to perform well in the classroom. We have, many times, given students B's on papers that deserved C's, simply because those students have made themselves known in class and have given us some stake in their success. If their classroom behavior has shown engagement, attentiveness, and preparedness (merely shown these qualities, mind you, not necessarily possessed them—we don't expect miracles), then when we come to their essays we're already thinking this person works at a different level than the average student (and so her grade will likely be higher than the average student's).

A professor, like most human beings, is a needy thing (particularly when sitting under the spotlight in the classroom setting). Exploit this. You might even manage to put your professors in the position where they seek admiration or sympathy from you. Some professors will look to a student to support their own (perhaps deluded) sense of themselves—that they are young, hip, radical, a sex-god(dess), whatever. Now, we would never suggest you cross that line between the development of familiarity and the risk of personal compromise, but there are subtle ways to provide the kind of feedback your professors seek without ending up in their bed (or worse yet, having them end up in your bed—there's nothing sadder than a professor skulking out of a dorm hallway at 5:00 a.m.). Human beings all look to others to support our images of ourselves, and tend to gravitate toward those people who provide this support. As always, there is a line between support and brown-nosing—you want to be artful but never reveal the artifice. If a professor smells insincerity or sucking-up, then you'll never be bread again, because you're toast. Instead, you need to be fantastically cool. You should do all things as if they were entirely natural. Affectation, the signs of force or effort, should be completely eliminated, so that each movement is conducted with grace and the appearance of sincerity. The out-of-classroom encounter will provide much of the opportunity for this kind of interaction, but there are also subtle things you can do to be a familiar and comforting presence in the classroom.

Be aware that all of this can be taken too far, and you have to measure your behavior according to feedback from your professor. If you choose to make yourself familiar by being interruptive, argumentative, and confrontational during lectures, then, when it comes time to assign our discretionary grade, yes, we'll know who you are, but, man, will we be gunning for you. Professors can easily find something within your work that they can use to justify their desire to punish you for their personal (and sometimes petty) dislike of you. Even if participation grades are not an explicit factor in your final grade, your actions in the class will play a role in the calculation. If you set yourself in opposition to the professor from Day One, then your work will have to be twice as good as that of other students just to get the same grade!

So we're obviously talking here about a certain kind of familiarity: the right kind—you want your professors to remember you because they like you, to not cringe every time that you open your mouth. Remember, it doesn't matter if you end up in the classroom of the worst professor in the institution—that's who's going to be filling in that space marked Final Grade. So here are a few things you might do in the classroom to influence the number that your professor's pen scribbles next to your name.

ATTENDANCE

As far as showing up for class, as the famous running-shoe slogan says, Just Do It! This is one place where you have to bite the bullet, particularly those of you in upper-level courses. Okay, so maybe professors who routinely lecture to over three hundred students will have a bit of trouble noticing your daily presence, but you'd be surprised what they do notice. Students routinely sit in the same places, and, from the front of the room, it is easy to discover that a particular row has an oddly different character— the professor will think about it for a second, and it may not hit him until his butt hits the office chair, but suddenly he will remember, "Hey! Dianne wasn't at my lecture on *Great Expectations*. Dammit!" And God help Dianne if she doesn't make it to the next class because that impression will be very difficult to plaster over. You'd be surprised at how much professors can remember about attendance patterns without even consciously trying.

You've got to understand that most professors are essentially insecure about our own abilities and ourselves as people. The success or failure of our most recent lecture will determine how we feel about ourselves for the rest of the day (pathetic, yes, but honest). Lectures are a reflection of our personalities, and we often think of them as suggestive of our competence in a given area— so we have quite a lot invested in them and your response to them. It matters to us that we got a laugh at a certain joke in class, or that students seemed genuinely engaged in the topic on a certain day (or, at least, that they stayed awake most of the time). If you don't want your transcript to reflect the psychoses of your professor, tell her she is worth listening to (even if she is not) by showing up.

When you show up at lectures on a consistent basis, your professor reads this as interest not only in the course but in herself. It is a kind of loyalty and will be rewarded as such. Professors are always willing to take certain things as compliments (anything except compliments)—so when, class to class, you are there on time and waiting to hear the pearls of wisdom they're about to lay before you, they will choose to interpret this as an indication that you enjoy hearing them and that you like them as people. Again, this positively predisposes them toward you, so when they see your work or come to your name on the list there will be a flash of recognition: "This student is engaged and insightful (because she likes my work). Her work will probably be top notch." People—and professors are almost people—want to think good things about themselves, so if you provide them with the raw material to do so (your interest in and attention to them) then they'll take it to heart—and some of that interest and attention will be returned to you. Attendance, day in and day out, is one of the most important ways you express this interest.

Now, of course, there is a little flexibility here. You'll need to determine your professor's expectations of the class. In our experience, the older, dustier kind of professor is less interested in the exchange between instructor and student. This professor thinks he's seen it all; teaching is getting a little tired. Each morning he goes to his filing cabinet and pulls out the notes for today's topic. The notes are yellowed with age (they were written long before you were born), chewed around the edges, and you get the feeling that if a breath of fresh air ever managed to come into the classroom, the notes would dissolve into vapor right there on the lectern, along with the professor. If your professor rarely lifts his head from his notes, leaves no room for questions or discussion, and conceives of lectures as a period of dictation, then skipping out to the pub now and then will likely leave your reputation undamaged. However, some of these old puppies have pretty fragile egos and vindictive spirits; as with everything, use careful judgment, and measure your professor's commitment to teaching.

But when you find yourself in a class in which the professor is under 45 and/or uses words like "interactive" and "decentered" (or even mentions out loud the notion of a "teaching model" or, worse yet, "pedagogical philosophy") then you'd better plan on being at every class. Know the signs: if this professor is one of those who asks questions and scans the room patiently waiting for responses, then don't miss her classes (not only for the recognition factor, but because those questions, taken together, will likely be important when that professor comes to set the final exam—they might, in fact, be the only things from the lecture that you should write down). In the case of such professors, graduate school might not be far enough in their past that they have forgotten what it is like to sit there for 50 to 100 minutes, so you might even get an apology once in a while from the lectern. ("I know this is tough going, but I want to establish the background here—there's not much more.")

This is the kind of professor you have to play the most carefully because she tends to be self-conscious about what she does. These professors will be trying very hard to produce lectures (they don't yet have the files of yellowed paper that the older guy has, though their pages may be in the process of yellowing), and they will be hoping that the material they do produce is titillating and innovative (possibly even "subversive"—yawn). They want to walk down the halls and think that they are well liked by their students (and perhaps even feared by the "establishment" for their "radical" tendencies). This kind of professor is the easiest to exploit. And giving these professors the appearance of loyalty, interest, engagement, and admiration (through regular attendance and even pretending to be a disciple) will set you in a good position to charm some A+ grades out of them.

Often the clothes and presentation of professors will give you insight into the ways in which they see themselves, and, correspondingly, the ways in which they see their teaching. Black jeans (oh hell, jeans of any color)—especially if the jeans are worn with a tweed jacket or some such ridiculous get-up, an earring in a man's ear or multiple earrings in the case of a woman, a bad spiked haircut about a decade too young for him, Birkenstocks with dark socks—all these can be taken as clues to the way in which this professor wants to be seen and regarded.

This professor is self-conscious about being associated with the older ones with the power; it's like an early midlife crisis in which he tries desperately to connect himself with youth. It is also an attempt to make a statement, to anyone who will listen, saying, "Hey, just 'cause I'm in the same department doesn't mean I'm one of these dusty old farts; I'm a free-thinking individual who is sexually and politically active." These professors will probably see teaching as an extension of their political mission; they'll want to enlighten their class with radical thought. So, to them, attendance counts, though they would never admit it—it would make them feel too "authoritative" and "conventional." (The guy who wears the denim shirt with a tie, well, you need to be a little more careful with him—he's playing the middle of the road.)

Think as well about how your professor addresses the class: standing behind a lectern? Sitting on top of a desk, with feet dangling? Pacing madly, making eye contact only to silence opposition? Sitting defensively behind a big oak desk? These aspects of demeanor are also telling. He may be trying to create a certain casual atmosphere, or suggesting a certain "hipness"—read these signs and give feedback accordingly. The casual atmosphere is often a façade beneath which lurks someone desperate to be taken seriously. All of these types keep a careful eye on attendance because, to them, it reflects their success.

However, if you do need to miss some classes, make your professor aware of the circumstances and express regret for your necessary absence. Do this as soon as possible after the absences; don't wait, like some students do, until the end of the course—by then, the professor's impression of you is locked. And do it carefully: too much information (like the details of your rectal examination) will alienate you; not enough will make professors think you're faking it. Never say you were too busy! Part-time work, hobbies, or the demands of another course are the last things you want to claim interfered with your ability to fulfill your responsibility to your professor's course. These excuses immediately set you up in the professor's mind as a poor time-manager and perhaps a student uncommitted to (or, worse, unsuited for) scholarly endeavor. She will also realize, through these excuses, that she is not at the top of the list of your priorities, which is where she feels she should be.

If there's been a death or a serious illness, let her know in one short apology: "I'm sorry I missed class on Thursday; my grandmother died. I got some notes from Cheryl though." At that point you're likely to get a look of great sympathy and an assurance not to give it another thought—you may even get an inquiry about your condition. These moments require strength though; don't break down in front of the professor because most professors don't know how to deal with it, and not knowing what to do will make them very uncomfortable. The out-of-class conference or the after-class swarm will be the place for the relating of this information, and the professor will tell you, through body language and verbal clues, when you've said enough and when to go on. Read the signs.

Also remember that professors have been students. They can sniff out a false excuse like a pig sniffs our truffles. Your reasons for absences need to be clear and brief and watertight because if a professor thinks you're lying, that impression will be more damaging than never having offered an excuse. Professors tend to become a little suspicious after that same grandmother's fourth or fifth unfortunate demise during a single school term. You would be amazed at how detrimental essay deadlines can be to a grandparent's health.

It may sound like a drag to have to go to each and every class, but let us assure you that the nature of the relationship it can establish with your professor will be well worth the loss of a few sleep-ins. Remember that your professor has to show up for every class (and the professor has to—well, is supposed to—show up well prepared for each session), and so she will have very little sympathy for absences due to beauty sleep. Attendance signifies a great deal in the professor's mind, and the commitment you prove through your attendance will make the professor committed to you as well.

IN YOUR FACE

Something such as where you sit in the classroom might not seem all that important, but it is. In your simple choice of seat you are positioning yourself in relation to your professor and, in some instances, this might determine your in-class relationship. Are you wallpaper, or are you up front to be counted (and counted in)? Again, on the first day of class, you'll need to do some investigative observation. Does this professor have a preferred side of the room? Most professors do—find out which side that is, and sit there. (For us, it is often the side that the window is on: by the window, there is usually a ledge to lean on, and one can take long pensive looks outside—while appearing very thoughtful—and compose an answer or the next golden nugget of wisdom.)

Many professors will determine their favorite side based on the arrangement of students in the room: if there are few students on a given side, then a professor is likely to favor the more populated area. One particular part of the room might be the frequent home of the most expressive group of students—scout out your classmates to determine who are the speakers. Professors will gravitate toward the source of visual cues (nods and smiles and attentive glances). Visual cues are reassuring, and we like to be reassured. Some professors will choose a group of "default" or "go-to" students (those they will rely on when no one else is speaking). So you need to figure out quickly where the wallpaper section of the room is, and avoid it. Place yourself within the focus of the professor—some students seek to avoid this area and thus avoid any undue attention (like directed questions), but better you should be among the targets than the ignored.

Do your professors pace when they lecture? If so, this gives you a little more room in which to position yourself. Never sit at either extreme of the pace route (the point where the professor turns). The pacing professor is usually composing his words on the fly and at the turn will be focusing more on getting back to the lectern for another glance at the notes. If you're at that pivot point, you're likely to be overlooked.

This goes for blackboard space as well; never sit at either extreme of the blackboard. The professor has a kind of tunnel vision; conceive of the classroom as a Roman coliseum—you want to sit where the blood is going to spatter. From the professor's position there is a kind of blank space that takes the shape of an inverted U—this is where you'll find the wallpaper (all along the sides and up along the back). The periphery of the room will be peripheral in the mind of the professor. Think about the visual field of the professor (watch the way she scans the classroom), and place yourself well within the extremes of her sight-lines.

Once you have determined the side of the room to sit on (the favorite side), you'll want to place yourself within the second or third row from the front. The second row is probably the best place to be—this way, you won't be looked over by a professor who prefers to stand and deliver, you won't crowd the professor like the in-your-face, front-row people, and you won't be missed by the professor too insecure to look very far from his notes. What you're seeking out here is the position for eye contact. You want to be one of those who provide the nods and looks of interest because this is how you worm your way into his heart. During the course of any lecture even the most self-engrossed professor will look up to see how the material is being received; when he does, you want to be in the position of his gaze, responding as if his words are the most important revelation that you have ever heard. Leave anonymity for the wallpaper, and get in your professor's sight and mind.

TAKING AN INTEREST

With this visibility, though, there comes a certain responsibility. Your professors want their ideas reinforced, not critiqued; you've got to be the one to look engaged, sometimes pensive, and always as if their words are causing an intellectual reaction in you, making you think. It would be wonderful if this were always a natural response, but, okay, 45 minutes on the decline of the peanut plantation and its effect on the gross national product of Brazil might not provide the kind of material that you'll want to repeat on a first date (though it might complement nicely the spinach leaf caught between your front teeth). But your professor, the one spewing this stuff, thinks she's onto something here, and, to play the game, you have to meet her enthusiasm with something other than indifference. You have no idea how important it is that you laugh at her jokes, or show the right degree of astonishment at her claims. The goal here isn't to make the professor feel better; that's merely the means. The goal is controlling the subjective aspect of the grade, which that professor will produce. The subjective zone, that little gray area that might mean the difference between a C and a B, or a B and an A, can depend on the ways in which you respond—as wallpaper, an unchanging pattern providing a background, or as a reactive surface, responding to and registering the professor's desperate appeal for interest.

DAVID: Several years ago, I had one student who was at every class and who sat right up under my nose. She put herself in a great position for recognition. But she didn't realize, or didn't care, that this was also the position I would look to for my own appraisal of success or failure—I invested my sense of self-worth as a lecturer/teacher in her, and her reactions partially determined my sense of the way things had gone and the quality of my material. All this because she sat in a certain place.

Failing to realize this, each class she sat with her book closed, her pen down, and her chin held in her hand, her elbow leaning on top of her desk. It becomes impossible for the professor to look at this kind of behavior and not take it as a reflection of self-worth. And the trouble is, the professor is a vindictive animal and, intentionally or not, they will take out their frustrations on their perceived sources.

This student became the focus of all my insecurities, and with each class that I looked on her apathetic, even hostile, face, I grew more resentful. If you think that this resentment didn't register in her grading, if you think that professors as a group are above such petty exercises of power, and if you think I could separate the person's work from the person's presence in my mind, then I've got this little package of real estate in Florida that I'd like to talk with you about.

Your professor is someone who thinks that he has something to say; that's why he's a professor (and that is why he's spent the best ten years of his life becoming the "expert" on the history of eunuchs in China in the twelfth century while everyone else on the planet was having fun, having kids, and taking vacations). And every speaker needs a listener. Speakers will invest a whole lot of themselves in someone who listens to them—the world is full of people trying to have their say, trying to shout above the din. The professor is one of these people. But the professor has the added advantage of a captive audience; she is the one to assign the grades. So you're captive, but are you captivated? Well, maybe not, but you'd better look it. It's a matter of body language.

BODY TALK

From across the crowded bar, you notice a beautiful woman (you may substitute this sex designation according to your own fantasies). She is looking directly at you, and her mouth moves sheepishly toward a smile. From her position facing the bar, she slowly turns her body in your direction, one arm resting on the side of the stool, the other draped casually on the bar, her fingertips caressing the damp, cool surface of her tall glass. Though these actions speak volumes—at least they might to Dr. Freud—this would not be the kind of stuff you'd want to import into the classroom situation. But there is a body language appropriate for the non-wallpaper student, and though it shares little else with the seduction scenario, like that behavior, it is intended to suggest that you're interested.

Think of the classroom as a theater; the professor is the actor and you are her audience. Actors can give bad performances, but they are more likely to blame their troubles on a bad audience: "Man, they were dead out there tonight!" We're not suggesting that you deliver a standing ovation after each lecture, but you're not going to score points by snoring in your seat or walking out in the middle of Act 2. Some professors deliver monologues: long, self-generated meditations on the day's topic. These instructors are more difficult to respond to—there'll be less room to make your presence felt. (Professors whose lectures are based in discussion and interaction, though, are practically telling you what they want from you.)

One colleague of ours, who shall remain nameless, had a prepared script each day, which she read to the assembled students— admiration for the dedication required to produce such a document for each class was checked only by sympathy for the poor students who had to endure it. But there they were, a room full of students (understandably) bordering on comatose. Though the students were justified in their boredom, this professor thought that she was doing the right thing for her students—and this is where the conflict arises. A professor is usually (though not always) well intentioned toward students, and when those good intentions are met with looks of intense boredom and suffering, then the professor gets frustrated (or worse, bored), and the individuals in the class pay a very high price (both in the lecture and on the grade sheet). However, in our colleague's class, there were a couple of students who were playing it well.

Playing it well simply means being a good listener. This might require an extra gallon of coffee before class. The key is not to treat the classroom like a telephone call, where you can pick your toes and scratch yourself at will (or where you put the receiver down and have a snack while your long-winded friend is still blathering on).

The classroom might be large, but the professor is small; the class may have many students, but there is usually only one professor—to him, what's happening in the room is personal. You should try to conceive of the lecture as personal contact (whether your professor makes it seem personal or not). If you think of the classroom experience as a one-to-one conversation with the professor, then you will be more likely to give the kind of feedback that encourages a stronger relationship with the professor—you will find that a kind of intimacy will develop between you and the professor. Trust us, your individuality might be compromised, but it is not lost in the apparent anonymity of the classroom. A professor will notice her environment. Even the most awkward lecturer eventually manages to lift her eyes from the page, and when she does, she is seeking reinforcement, someone to provide the visual cues suggesting that things are okay and she can go on with confidence. Just give your professor a slow thoughtful nod, a forward movement of the upper body and head suggesting more intent listening, or a direct look—whatever it might be, it is an acknowledgment to the speaker that you are interested in her material.

The student who provides this support, this suggestion of interest, will become a focal point for the professor. The professor will like seeing this student in her classroom day to day because this responsive person provides comfort and security, a safe place to look class after class, and this student will be rewarded for this attention not only because really listening will better prepare him for papers and exams, but because this student will receive the benefit of the doubt whenever the professor has to put a grade next to his name.

This comfort factor applies also for the more discussion-oriented professor—but this professor will require more than silent support from you. He is going to ask you to prove you've been listening, and you're going to have to take one of the opportunities he offers to do so. With this professor, at least once a class, you must answer a question, ask a question, or participate in a discussion with a comment. This professor wants to hear your voice, and it is your job to figure out how best to make your voice heard. Depending on the nature of the course, the professor might even ask for volunteer readers; this is a really cheap, nonthreatening way for you to step out front. Your participation will make him think that he is successful in his attempt to reach you, which, in a self-flattering and roundabout way (you are of course taking the route directly through his ego), ultimately makes him think better of you (you become, to his thinking, the student who "gets it" and who appreciates his "genius").

ASKING A QUESTION

In *The Book of Laughter and Forgetting*, Milan Kundera suggests that love is constant interrogation. What Kundera is getting at is that asking questions of someone suggests your interest in them. By Kundera's advice, if you want to pick someone up at a party, don't talk about yourself; instead ask them all about themselves. Now, you don't have to love your professors, nor do they need to love you, but a well-phrased and well-timed question can enhance these relationships also.

A question from a student is always a welcome event, but there are questions that work for you in terms of your relationship with the professor, and questions that work against you. The discussion-oriented professor loves it when you ask a question because it gives her a moment to appear helpful, open, casual, and interested. It also makes the class conform to her notion of the interactive, sharing experience. Questions to the dictation-oriented professor need to be handled and timed more carefully. Moderation is a rule in either case—don't ask more than two questions in a row, and don't ask the same question over and over. You must remember that in some sense a question is always a statement: some professors will welcome the chance to dazzle you with their brilliance in responding effortlessly to your unexpected question; others might fear the question for its potential to compromise their control or even to undermine their authority. Once again, you'll need to read your professors to time and phrase your question in such a way that you will always enable them to show what they know, not look like fools revealing their ignorance.

In your carefully chosen seat, you're pretty visible (that was the idea, right?), so you shouldn't have to work too hard to get the attention of the professor. Some professors want to encourage a casual atmosphere and are happy when they think that they've made students comfortable enough simply to break in at an opening without putting their hand up. In a room where you are competing for attention with some other savvy students, you might have to put your hand up at the same time as you begin expressing your question, or you might want to look for ways to jump into the discussion that look natural, engaged, and effortless. The more conservative (usually older) professors will want and wait for that hand flying in the air—they'll read it as a sign of respect.

If you've got something to ask, and you should try to find something to ask (remember, it will be read as a sign of your interest and engagement), wait for a break. If the professor is on a roll, tripping forward, spewing forth, and spitting all over the people in the front row, then you're going to piss him off if he has to stop before he has made that brilliant point he was working toward. When there's a pause (but not when the professor is mid-sentence), get his attention. If you're not in his sight-line at the moment, you might need a low, unthreatening "uh, excuse me." If this guy's really steaming ahead and doesn't seem to be at all interested in being interrupted, then write your question down and put an asterisk by it. Come back to it when there is an appropriate moment, or maybe in the next class—or bring it to him in the after-class swarm around the podium.

Never ask a question in the last three minutes of class time, unless questions are called for by the professor (and, even here, weigh the sincerity of the request—if nobody asks one, is he going to go on, or will the class be over? If it's a case of the former, then ask away, but if the class was going to end if not for your question, then hold it like a full bladder on a crowded airplane—nobody, especially not the professor, likes students who lack the ability to recognize that they are prolonging the class when everyone else is brain-dead). Professors are not always being genuine when they ask for questions—some simply use the phrase "Are there any questions?" as a lead in to "Well, if there are no questions, then I'll see you next time."

DAVID: I had a professor like this once, and every time he'd ask his wrap-up question, one particular student would go flipping (audibly) through her notes looking for something to ask. Her question was an obvious attempt to perform, to have her voice heard, and to appear intelligent, and the animosity this student gained by asking her question could be read in the eye rolling and groans of students and professor alike as they watched the clock move past the assigned class time and into its fourth hour. Who knows, this student might even have been raising genuinely important issues—but her timing was so off that we were only hearing our stomachs grumble and feeling our collective annoyance.

A question is a performance, but the professor is the leading player in this theater, and if you try to upstage him, then you might just find yourself on the wrong end of a Quentin Tarantino movie with somebody about to go medieval on your ass. Play your hand with subtlety. Know that there is always a certain amount of trepidation in the professor when he is being asked a question—he wants to be able to answer it and thus enhance his sense of his own expertise. Your question should not be phrased as a direct challenge, even if it is. You should, by all means, express opposing views, but this requires tact, not aggression. And let's just put this one to bed: you don't need to point out to a professor that he left a letter out of a word when he wrote it on the blackboard—it'll likely be clear to everyone in the room what was intended, and so your drawing attention to the error does nothing for anyone and may be read, by a particularly insecure professor, as an attempt to embarrass.

Always try to feed a question out of the professor's line. If a professor is talking about one thing, see if you can relate it to another thing that has been addressed that class. During a discussion of, for example, effective subway advertising, you might come up with, "Does what you suggested about the effect of subway advertising apply to all forms of outdoor public advertising, or does the underground environment make the subway a special case?" Something like this achieves multiple goals: it tells the professor you've been listening, it tells her you've been thinking about and processing the information by attempting to apply it, and it leaves room for the confirmation to come from the professor. This is much preferable to "The subway's not so different from other modes of public transport—the advertising would achieve the same effect in any environment." Framed as a statement, this attempt leaves no room for the professor and so might be interpreted as a direct challenge rather than a contribution that is constructive and productive.

Students who begin questions with (and we've heard this opener way too many times) "I haven't finished reading this yet, but . . ." should be taken out and shot because they are committing suicide anyway. Another question of this kind is "I wasn't at the last class, so I don't know if this was already covered, but . . ." Questions like these draw attention to their own basis in ignorance—why would you do this? You might as well just hand the professor a note on the first day that says, "I'm very stupid, please place me in the bottom range when grading." And then there is our personal favorite, "I could be wrong, but . . ." You would be amazed how many people begin every comment they make in class like this; if you begin every question with a reference to your own ignorance, your professor will only see you as ignorant—you must try to show a little confidence (whether it is genuine or not) so that the professor starts to feel that the question is being asked by an admirable (and thoughtful) thinker who deserves an answer. And construct questions that are based on something you do know or that you did read—even if it is only last week's chapter or the five pages you managed to squeeze in between "Frasier" and "ER."

Create a question that tells the professor you are trying to establish connections between the current topic of study and the stuff you've already covered. Before the class, you might even plan something to ask (though you must make it appear spontaneous—there is nothing as impressive as a student who seems to be engaged in a dialogue). Maybe you read only Chapter 3 when you were assigned Chapters 3 to 7; if so, construct a question based on a very specific area within the part you've covered: "In Chapter 3, when Miller talks about cosmic dancing, is he using that phrase metaphorically, or is he suggesting that they really believed in that kind of thing?" Again, the question achieves multiple goals: it uses the terms of the particular course, applies them, and suggests that you're grappling with the material. Because a question speaks volumes to the professor about your level of engagement with the subject and her class, asking is telling, and you must tell her you're not wallpaper.

CALL ANSWERING

We are all familiar with the horrid and uncomfortable moment that follows a professor's question to the class—both sides of the podium feel it: the professor is looking desperately for someone (anyone with a pulse) to break the terrible and seemingly eternal silence; the students are trying as hard as possible to become invisible, to become one with their textbooks, and for God's sake *not* to meet the desperate professor's searching gaze. So how grateful do you think everybody is, especially the professor, if there is someone out there willing to take a shot at the question to defuse this tension? Always try to be this someone.

This does not mean you should try to be that student who is always putting in his two cents (often the precise worth of the contribution). What it means is that at least once a class (and no more than three times), you can be looked to for a thoughtful answer or comment. You are capable of formulating such a contribution, particularly if you're pressuring yourself for only one answer per class. If you read only Chapter 3 and you were supposed to have read to Chapter 9, then grasp your moment in the spotlight when the chance comes up.

The more organized professor may tell you in advance what she is planning for the focus of the discussion for the next class (though most of us stay barely a class ahead); with this prof you can actually know what to think about, and this will enable you to plan your participation. But, whether the professor tells you in advance what's coming or flies by the seat of her pants, questions rarely come from left field: three classes with her will likely show you the kinds of questions you can expect—prepare for those questions. Does this professor tend to focus on issues of gender, sexuality, politics, race, morals, and so forth? Is the rhythm or structure of this professor's class similar from week to week? Does she begin with a general overview of the readings and then focus in on a particular problem as an example? What are the kinds of things that this professor had revealed to you about her interests? Focusing on these tendencies, you might be able to anticipate questions that might be asked from class to class. This will take some analysis on your part at the beginning of the course, but you will be rewarded for this early effort throughout the year.

When you do decide to answer a question, avoid the one-word answer. Very few professors actually prepare a perfectly timed lecture; many over-prepare, but most feel slightly underprepared when they walk into the room. Our preparation style is fairly typical: for a fifty-minute class, we will go into the classroom with a couple of pages of notes, which, if they were just read without ad libbing and developing, would last about six minutes. Though a professor might suggest he asks questions to involve you actively in the learning process, asking questions is also, practically speaking, a technique a professor uses to stretch out the hour—to make him look as though he prepared a lot more material than he actually has. Sometimes class time moves very slowly for us too, you know, and let us tell you, you feel it a lot more painfully when you're the one expected to fill that time. But whether the professor asks questions to draw out class time or to try to involve his students, a one-word answer is seen as more of a hindrance than anything else (for one thing, it is hard for a rewarding class discussion to emerge out of an answer of "ya"). And, perhaps most importantly, it doesn't give you the stage time necessary to make that good impression on the professor.

Professors will often ask their questions badly (they will know it and so will you), and you need to be able to recognize these instances and use them to your advantage. A professor may ask a "yes or no" question; if she does, never give her back the simple "yes" or "no" answer. Chances are the professor just phrased the question poorly and really wanted a more comprehensive answer. So, in your answer, suggest why "yes" or why "no." And more often than not, the moments just before the question was asked will provide you with the material to develop such an answer.

Remember that the mind of the professor is the same as the mind of a real person, and there is usually some logical connection between his fragments of speech. For example, the professor may be talking about a particular issue (A) when something about what he has just said will trigger the idea that this is a good time for him to ask a question (B); to answer, you just need to figure out the connection (the gap between A and B). How did what he said the moment before provoke the question in his mind? Was it a particular word or category? Thinking of the lecture process as a conversation will help you; you can usually chart a choppy conversation all the way back to its beginning just by finding the bridges that took you from topic to topic. This is true of the path of a lecture also, so the process is not as mysterious as it seems, and questions do not come out of thin air. If the professor has been lecturing on, say, the Oedipal complex, and later asks a banal, "yes or no" question about the child's early learning skills, you might answer "yes" or "no" and then refer back to the point about the Oedipal complex—you have anticipated the connection, and the discussion will follow nicely from there, much to the professor's relief (and your future advantage).

But remember, though you do need to be seen as willing to engage in the classroom questioning dynamic, don't feel you should answer every question. Sure, you can be the one to whom the professor might turn in the face of silence, but don't try to overplay this angle and monopolize the moments when the professor opens up to the room.

HARRY: A few years ago, I had a student who, every time I paused or asked a question, would try to interject his brilliance. This became so irksome that my class, as a collective, conspired to protest and came to see me about him. But they needn't have bothered; he was so thoroughly under my skin that I'd already begun to scratch.

Read the signs: if your hand's up for the third time and a professor says, "Let's give someone else a chance" or "How about somebody who hasn't answered yet today," then back off immediately.

Try to speak, answering or asking, between one and three times each class. If you can't answer a question during the class, then you'd better ask one (asking is easier than answering and can often be just as effective).

AT THE LAST MINUTE

We said, in the section on asking a question, never to ask in the last three minutes of class. Here's why: the psychology of the professor is such that, at the beginning of the class, he is feeling rich in time (he might even be concerned about his ability to fill all those minutes), and so he's very willing, even desirous, to elaborate points, stretch things out, and pursue seemingly insignificant stuff. But as the last minutes approach and the professor becomes increasingly aware of his imminent loss of the stage, he finally has to get to the point of the discussion once and for all.

These are the moments when professors panic and think about how what we've been blabbing about for the last two hours will be useful to you all. As fidgety students begin to rattle their papers and shuffle to leave (don't do that—we hate that—we know we're out of time without these not-so-subtle hints), we feel like we're losing our grip on you, so we want to make sure you go away with what we had intended to give you, and we start spewing like a faucet. This might be the moment we give away an examination question or make connections between things that might help with an essay argument. In other words, if a professor is scrambling desperately to get something out at the last minute, you'd better believe it is something that you will have to know somewhere down the line.

So these are the minutes when, instead of asking a question, you should be listening carefully and writing down whatever is being said up there. These are also the minutes when those students around you, particularly the wallpaper, who are at that moment thinking about papering the walls of the classroom down the hall, will start to close books, pack their bags, rustle, and squirm. Don't follow their lead. To the professor, these can be the most important moments of the whole hour, and if he's had trouble getting a point across, this will be the moment when he will try to crystallize it—if he has been delaying, he will finally make the point clear at this moment. He may say he'll come back to it next class but don't count on this. Sit tight, listen carefully—better you should be a minute late for the next class or for lunch than miss these critical moments. Also, *never* be one of the paper rustlers: the desperate professor, knowing he's running out of time, is distracted by these rustlings and will often look at the offending student with hostility; the momentary event might seem insignificant, but a mental note has been made that might come back to haunt the rustler.

The dying minutes of the class are also a wonderful opportunity to display, by remaining focused while the rest of the class starts to disintegrate, your interest in the material (interest which, as we've said, the professor takes as a compliment). This might even be your way into (to be employed once only) the after-class swarm: "Sorry to bother you Professor Nelson, but I couldn't hear that last little bit about Shakespeare's use of humor. Would you mind repeating it for me?" A little halo goes "bing" up over your head, and you join the professor in a conspiratorial huddle within a world of deflectors and deserters. If the professor sees you as the one student desiring knowledge, this perception will provoke a protective instinct in him, and you will find yourself in this inner circle, treated differently.

THE AFTER-CLASS SWARM

This is that moment at the end of every class when the podium becomes magnetized. Up until this point in the class everyone has been doing everything possible to avoid and ignore that central position; now it becomes the hub of activity. Students are trying to book appointments and get back essays and assignments they should have picked up weeks a ago; they're asking for extensions on papers and answers to problems. The question for you: should I join in, or should I just leave?

The first thing you need to determine is whether or not your professor enjoys the after-class swarm, or whether she just wants to get the hell out of there. If the professor is one of those who is packing up her books as she finishes her last few sentences, then stay out of the swarm—by delaying this professor, you will frustrate her, and that will foster resentment. She might be meeting someone, she might have a kid to get home to, or she might be suffering from fatigue and a splitting headache after listening to her own voice for hours; whatever it is that is driving her out of the room, it's important to her. She is also likely thinking that she has set aside time for you (designated office hours) and that staying after class is extra work that she shouldn't have to do. We know the frustration of scheduling and waiting through three office hours a week, to which no one ever comes, only to be swamped with people at the end of a long lecture. The office-hour visit will ultimately be more effective than the after-class swarm in developing sympathy, familiarity, and confidence between professor and student (and that's what you're ultimately trying to accomplish).

As a general rule, if the professor is holding office hours directly after the class, then it is probably okay to swarm him at the podium for a short question. But if you really want to work something out, or you've got something that requires a little delicacy to express, then you're better off just going to his office rather than attempting to break through the hordes after class.

> **DAVID:** A student once came to me in the after-class swarm to tell me he was worried that his girlfriend was pregnant, and so he couldn't concentrate on a thing I had said. Truth be told, I didn't need to know either of these things, particularly his added confidence the next class when, with an immensely relieved look and a wink, he told me that this was his favorite time of the month.
>
> This is not the kind of interaction you want to initiate during the swarm (or ever, if you can avoid it).

The two of us have always rather enjoyed the swarm. There is a certain sense of frenetic adulation in being rushed by a crowd of undergraduates. Some professors, however, may find it too frenetic and a little intimidating, or they may have spent themselves during the lecture, and they want a little "down time." You can usually spot the cues; the professor who quickly gathers up all of her papers and doesn't look up as you approach will be looking for a clear way to the exit, and you shouldn't get in her way. On the other hand, the professor who lingers a little, shuffles papers without packing them away, and smiles at all comers likes the after-class swarm, and you would do well to be part of it. But within the swarm comes a certain anonymity that you have to overcome. The best way to work this will be through combining all the available opportunities: the after-class swarm, the office visit, and answering and asking questions.

But for the swarm in particular, when you get your turn up there, you must introduce yourself. The introduction is especially important at first; eventually professors will remember you, and, when they can address you by name, you're no longer wallpaper (well, it's a nice first step away at least). Just the first name will do; the rest can come with further contact. Also, a professor who knows your first name will be motivated to distinguish you from others that may have the same first name as you. Don't make it too elaborate, a simple "Hi, I'm Michael" will do, then quickly follow with your question. (Don't wait for an acknowledgment of the introduction, or that might seem to be the obvious goal of your approach.)

Your question should be asked with attention to the kind of impression you're trying to create. Remember, a question is really in many ways a statement, and the strength of a question will reflect on you. Appeal to the professor's expertise, but take the formality down a notch. Use all of the ideas discussed in the section on asking a question, and make the thing work for you: something like "Hi, my name is Sandra. I was wondering if you thought that Shakespeare was sympathetic to the Moor's position. I mean, if you're going to make somebody a tragic hero . . . then he has to be admirable as well, right?" Everything contained in the question will be stuff that you've considered in the context of the course; you'll just have tried to apply it in some new way. The presentation of the question should be fairly casual; this might even be the place to discuss a personal response to the subject— something like "You know, I couldn't help it, but the last chapter of this novel really made me angry" (as long as your comment is brief and there is room for response by the professor).

The after-class swarm is a burst of activity after a fairly regimented lecture session. Most of the students are going up there with a particular worry (late essays, poor grades, and so on) that would likely be better attended to in the office meeting. You will not want to be one of these people—you should come with a focused question that can be asked and answered in less than a minute, but that reveals that you have been thinking about the material. As you walk away offering thanks, and Clevis shoves his paper in the professor's face, asking how come he got such a low mark, you leave associated with the intellectual (the reason the professor became a professor in the first place), whereas old Clevis becomes an administrative problem (the bane of our existence as professors).

GET BACK

The classroom is also the place where the student often gets graded assignments back from the professor. You can master this event in two easy steps: take your paper and leave the room. No stopping to read the comments in the classroom, no glowering looks to the professor to try to telepathically intimidate him into a better grade. Professors hate giving graded work back in class; no one likes disappointing or damaging students' self-esteem. It spoils a successful lecture, and there is never a "right" time to do it. And if you react to a grade before you have absorbed the commentary, considered the critique, and generally acknowledged the work that the professor has put into grading it, then you really piss him off because he feels like he's wasted all the time he gave to the paper. If you stand in front of him after he hands it to you, flip to the last page, read the number that he has written, and start puffing and swelling, this will foster neither productive dialogue nor friendly relations. (Even if you have done well, professors do not want to hear your reaction to your grade right there in class.) Allow at least one day between the receipt of your assignment and approaching the professor for clarification or complaint. The next day the professor will not be feeling the overwhelming sense of anxiety that he felt while returning papers to 50 volatile undergraduates. The next day the professor will believe that you have taken the time to consider his position on the paper and that your response is intellectual rather than just a reflex. While you may think the meeting is about protesting a grade or solving a particular problem, it is also about creating a positive impression that will remain with the professor and affect his response to your work on future assignments.

SUMMARY

The amphitheater is full of students. The professor enters and takes her place at the podium. Looking out, she sees six students, pleasantly set off against a field of bland wallpaper. Partway through the lecture, a hand goes up; someone is struggling to break from the two-dimensional background. Be that somebody. Refuse to be wallpaper. Though the classroom may not be the most intimate setting, it is where the professor focuses most of the energy she devotes to the course. To become familiar here, to become a comforting and reliable presence, is to take mastery over the professor's subjective approach to your work; when she sits down to grade your material, you want her to meet it not with neutrality, certainly not with hostility, but with positive expectation. It's the classic self-fulfilling prophecy: your relationship with the professor makes her anticipate that you are a better-than-average student, and that anticipation actually influences how she grades your work. And it's probably the happiest vicious circle in which you'll ever get caught.

CHAPTER 4

Outclassed

SCHMOOZING YOUR PROFESSOR OUTSIDE THE CLASSROOM

Professors can seem a pretty intimidating breed, and the prospect of approaching them outside of class might be about as tempting as attending a Barry Manilow concert. And the vast majority of your professors, especially during the earlier years of your university career, will appear particularly unapproachable; they will seem to you to be lofty and in command of vast quantities of knowledge that you could never hope to possess. But it is time to demystify these professors and bring them down from that pedestal. If they know more than you, it is because they have been at it longer, not because they were born with the knowledge that they are throwing at the class, which is the same knowledge that they have thrown at countless classes before. You will figure this out by the end of your university career, but by then it might be too late to take advantage. In order to think about how you might play to win the professor and the university game, you need to start by reminding yourself that a professor is a human being with all the hang-ups, frailties, and problems of everybody else (chances are, though, they are less well-groomed).

UNMASKED

Picture yourself waking up one morning knowing that you have to stand before a university class and that you will be expected

65

to say something intelligent. Picture yourself scrambling desperately to find something to say that won't make you sound like a complete idiot. You are still exactly the same person that you have always been, but suddenly you must play the role of the intellectual, which fate or calling or poor career advice has set for you. If you can imagine this scenario, then you are imagining exactly what all your professors went through the first time they taught the course you are taking now (and some feel this every morning thereafter as well). We have not met a professorial colleague who, when teaching a course for the first time, did not end up reading some of the course material *for the first time* just a few hours ahead of their students.

You should know that there are times when your professors will arrive in class never having read the material in question from start to finish. They will only appear to have done so because you have brought with you to that class the assumption that they have done so, and that will be the only difference between you and them. Their bluff always succeeds because you, as students, project that assumption of intelligence onto them. Professors are more practiced at intellectual deception than you are—to get where they are, they have not only studied information, but they have also become experts in the science of faking knowledge when caught in a tight intellectual corner. A popular joke among English literature professors goes like this: "I would like to learn something about Tennyson. I think I'll teach a graduate course on him." Thinking of your professors in these human terms will make your approaches to them less awkward.

FIRST STRIKE

There are few experiences as intimidating as knocking on a professor's door for the first time. Chances are, you have arrived at college with some idea or myth about what this place represents. It is different, you assume, from the rest of society. While the rest of society works and plays and makes things like shirts and cars, this place thinks. And the result of that thinking is somehow supposed to alter the world. As you knock on the professor's door, you imagine that, on the other side of that door, there is a person in the process of forming some great thought that will influence future generations. Never have you felt so insignificant, so much out of your league.

What you do not know is that the person on the other side of the door is more likely to be cleaning his fingernails than in the midst of the formulation of the revolutionary and world-altering idea. The few "great thinkers" in society are not behind that door but in a dusty archive somewhere—they have not likely been in an undergraduate lecture theater since they were undergrads. Your professors, on the other hand, are just like everyone else, just like your own parents in fact. They are probably not tugging at their beard, drawing on their pipe, or trying to reinterpret some idea of social order (and if they are, chances are they are not getting very far). Instead, they are thinking of ways to kill time, and they're feeling bored. Or they are scrambling to prepare a class, and feeling frantic. Or they are grading a bad essay, and feeling annoyed. They are wondering what they are going to have for dinner, where they are going to buy their Pepto-Bismol, or whether they paid their phone bill that month.

PERSONAL ADS

Now that you know that your professor is just another Joe or Jill Shmoe trying to earn a living and get through the day, it is time to talk about why it is absolutely necessary that you find a way to approach your instructor outside of the classroom. The best opportunity to force your professors to take notice of you as a human being and not just as another number on a page is by talking with them outside the classroom. One-on-one contact is the only way to elevate your relationship with the professor.

The bigger your classes, the more difficult the prospect of getting that professor to know you. If you are sitting in the back row of a five-hundred-seat auditorium, there is even more urgency to forcing the professor to catch your eye, to know your name, and to remember your face and your voice and your ideas. The bigger the class (and the trend suggests that classes will continue to get bigger), the more you must try to be known. If it takes waiting in line, if it takes going out of your way to appear during her office hours, this is a sacrifice that you must make to elevate your status. The more the university system forces professors to stand before massive classes and speak at the multitudes through microphones, and the smaller the dot you become in the expansive auditorium before them, the more necessary humanizing yourself to them will become.

The process of approaching a professor, any professor, must be handled very carefully. Every professor is different and has a different tolerance level for well-intentioned students. Some professors have some spare time on their hands, during which they might want to talk about your ideas or their course or a movie or your plans for the summer. Your professor might seem to be the type that doesn't care about you as anything more than another head of cattle (and, under these circumstances, you must make still more of an effort to rise above that status). Some professors like to have their egos stroked, and some will see right through you if you try to flatter. Some professors would simply prefer to be left alone. In each case, there is a way to raise your professor's awareness of you. It's easy as pie to make them aware of you, but you want to cause that awareness in a positive way and have it work for you in a positive way.

At its best, the out-of-class situation offers you the ability to transcend your obvious role as student and to become a more fully developed individual in the professor's eyes. Once this out-of-class dialogue begins, the professor must cease to see you only in relation to the grind of the course, and must begin to take account of you as someone with a life—with family, friends, a future, and a past—more or less like his own or that of his children. You have to find some common ground: the course is obviously the first thing you have in common, but if you can extend this into the personal realm in some small way then you will force the professor to identify with you at a more human level. It is easy to give a D to a student number, but if the professor has some sense of you as a person with feelings and a personal investment, then that D is much harder to put beside your name.

The psychological effect of this new sympathetic awareness in the mind of the professor cannot be overestimated. If your professor knows you as a person, he cannot give you a poor grade without being forced to deal with the effect of that poor grade. He will not be able to give you a grade that might compromise your future, or a grade that might lower your sense of self-worth, without working through how he might also react to that same situation. Inevitably, it boils down to an issue of guilt; the more the professor is forced to sympathize with your position, the guiltier that professor will feel giving you the bad grade. If you have arrived at this degree of sympathy or guilt in your dealings with a professor, then you're in; you have managed the game successfully.

WRONG TURNS

There is also a wrong way to approach the out-of-class dynamic— a way that could lead to disaster. Despite your good intentions, your efforts to spend some time in a one-on-one situation with the professor could, if not handled properly, end up working against you. In fact, there are as many students who fail miserably in their attempt to approach the professor out of class as there are those who succeed. And if you annoy and alienate your professor, your behavior will definitely end up hurting your grade. Professors are ordinary creatures, and, being ordinary, they are not above petty reactions like spite and vengeance and making you pay just for being a dweeb or a pain in the neck.

We as professors can recall very few experiences more annoying than those instances of students becoming overly zealous in their efforts to approach us out of class. And these students usually start out very well in making a good impression, but fail to recognize where to draw the line.

HARRY: One student that I can recall began her out-of-class dialogue with me by calling me prior to the first class to ask about course readings so that she could get a head start. At this point, I admired her initiative. A few days later, she called again to talk at length about her responses to the works she had read. I found myself a little less enthusiastic. The next day (which was still weeks before the start of the course) she called again, asking me to list some essay topics so that she could get started on her written work. By this point, I rushed her off the phone, and for the next few weeks, I was forced to screen my calls.

Long before I stepped into the classroom, I knew that this

was someone to avoid, not despite her best intentions but specifically because of these intentions. In attempting to make me a sympathetic professor, she had failed to show any sympathy with my position, and, as a result, had permanently alienated me.

This is one, somewhat extreme, example of the wrong approach. Yet, there are far worse stories, bordering on the hellish or pathological, of students calling in the dead of night to tell a professor why their essay is going to be late, or of the student who stopped by a professor's apartment uninvited and unannounced just to borrow a blank computer disk and to give him a box of Reese's Pieces. If any of this sounds like something you might do in approaching your professor, then you had better read on.

You may begin to feel at some point as though your professor is a friend, but your professor, though occasionally friendly, is never a friend. A professor has power over you, in the sense that eventually she will be putting a number next to your name that is supposed to have some correlation with your worth in the world, and that will have some influence on your success in life. This is not the basis for any friendship. Regardless of the tone of your interaction with the professor, you must remember that you are guiding her in a specific direction. Your interaction with her is always a task, and that task is never to be mistaken for something as enjoyable as friendship.

SEARCHING FOR THE FOUNTAIN OF YOUTH

To assume that all professors can be approached in the same way is naive. There is no single stereotype to fit all professors. One must be wary, for example, of the young professor taking himself a little too seriously in an effort to gain credibility with students and peers, or of the older, jaded professor just riding out the final years before retirement. But, then, those professors in the middle can be varied and dangerous too. Whatever type of professor you encounter in your university career, you must approach that person with the awareness that it is your right to occupy some of his time in addressing, at the very least, academic matters. This awareness will establish the level of confidence you want to project (and the level of comfort), but it certainly has nothing to do with the level of aggression you should display. If you march into an instructor's office talking about your rights and your demands, you might just as well slip a blindfold over your eyes because you've just stepped in front of a firing squad. Yes, you have bought that time with good money and with personal sacrifice, but, in the interest of charming the professor (which is really in your own best interest), you may want to find ways of making him feel as though he is the one doing you the favor.

The student must be careful to approach humorless or stodgy professors on their own level, and that same clever student can learn to take advantage of the professors who are desperate to prove to the students how "hip" they are to the younger culture of the day. There is one thing that you should remember about professors: they are among the few people in society who get older and older while at the same time being condemned to spend their entire life around beautiful people in the prime of life. They are the only outdated people in a place of eternal youth. And that hurts. They will find themselves falling further and further behind in their knowledge of current trends, like a colleague of ours who, when a student compared the lyrics of a poem to those of Marky Mark, did not understand the reference, and has never forgiven himself.

The fact that your professors are painfully out of date can be effectively exploited; due to their circumstance, they are often desperate to keep up with the trends, and not be identified as old and "different." You can play on this, making them feel young and "with it." Nothing will make the ego of a professor grow more quickly than being made to feel that she, more than her colleagues, is considered cool by the younger generation. And if you are the one to promote this ego growth, well, you'll also be the one to harvest its rewards.

The point is to be able to size up the professor and deal with that person on his own level. This will take a certain amount of insight on the part of the student, particularly if the professor is the type of person who does not allow his personality (presuming he actually has one) to surface in the classroom. You should allow the professors themselves to dictate the terms on which they will be addressed. Usually this will not take a great deal of time. Students should already, from the classroom experience, have some idea of the personality type they are dealing with. If the professor rarely appears interested in the comments that students make in class, then that person will likely not have a great deal of patience for you out of class either, and you should probably try to find a way to get to the point of your visit as soon as possible. If the professor does appear in class to be sympathetic to the students' point of view, then there may be more room to build up a personal rapport.

Generally, when you approach the professor outside of the classroom, two things can happen: you're welcomed in or you're hurried out. In the latter case, the professor, either by nature or by necessity, will have little or no time for you. You should be prepared for this situation, even if the professor initially appeared to be the type of person who would have invited leisurely conversation. Professors are a particularly moody and inconsistent bunch, and you might have the bad luck of catching even the nicest-seeming professor in the middle of a crisis.

One good rule to follow is never to knock on a professor's door shortly before she is about to go teach your class. Chances are, she's either working to get her thoughts together, or else she is in edgy anticipation, and so she'll not be as receptive to your sudden intrusion. After-class meetings are also tricky. You should not forget that a lecture is a performance, and, as much as it takes your professor time to get up for the performance, it also takes time to come down. The professor might be energetic and chatty after a lecture, but the conversation might have little effect, as the professor's mind is often just racing blindly and frantically at that point.

In the case of the professor who is preoccupied with preparations or other matters, you will know not to push the interview too far. The professor will immediately challenge the student to get to the point of the visit with some statement like "Yes, what is it?" or "What can I do for you?" If this kind of urgency is enforced upon you, the best answer is "If you are busy, I would be happy to come back at a better time." (This utterance, in fact, might be a good way to begin every conversation with a professor outside of the classroom. The professor will appreciate your consideration and probably give you the time you want.) If, when the door is opened for you, the professor has a worried and hunted look, it is best to beat a hasty and graceful retreat.

COFFEE TALK

If, upon hearing your offer to come back at a better time, the professor still wants you to remain, you must gauge whether you misread the professor's initial response, or whether she wants you to discuss the purpose of your visit now, but very quickly. This is why, in approaching your professor, you should always arrive prepared to articulate the reason for your visit in one very brief question.

What you must understand is that one of the things professors hate the most is the feeling that they are merely entertaining a student who is bored and looking to kill some time, or that the student is obviously just taking up time for the sake of forcing the professor to notice him. Don't open with general questions that go nowhere, such as "I was wondering if I could talk about the essay?" or "I was wondering if I could just ask one question about today's lecture?" Always suggest that there is one pressing issue in your work that cannot wait any longer for the professor's attention, like a problem understanding one specific section of the course work, or one specific aspect in your essay or exam preparations. Make sure that the problem with which you approach your professor is as intelligent and challenging a problem as possible, since the intelligence of the question will reflect on you and dictate how she will judge you from that point onward. If you noticed that the professor was having some problem explaining a specific issue in class, that topic is a good place to start (but don't draw attention to the professor's difficulty). Don't forget that this meeting is a performance, and that you will establish a lasting impression in the first minute.

But there are other specific issues you can raise to engage your professor for the first time without seeming to be a nuisance or simply a time waster. If you have no further insights to offer to the ideas that were presented in class discussion, then certainly you can think of a specific question to ask about the design of the course as a whole, the reason why topics are included or omitted, or the logic behind the order in which the material is being presented. (Of course, this must never be phrased in such a way that would allow the professor to think that you are challenging her authority. You must make it clear that you are interested in the course only to the extent that you want to know more about it.)

If you have no questions to ask on the design of the course, then remark on one aspect of the course that was particularly meaningful to you, and ask if the professor might possibly be willing to recommend further readings on the subject. (This will not only introduce you to the professor, but identify you as someone who is willing to engage in independent thought, thereby suggesting to the professor that you are probably A-level material.) You might ask the professor to clarify a comment scribbled upon an assignment, or to suggest how you might address the problem in future assignments. You might ask the professor if he is teaching any other courses the following semester, thus stroking his ego and letting him know that he'll likely be dealing with you again in the future. You might also ask him if he saw an article in a newspaper or magazine that relates in some way to the course topic, and ask what he thought of the article. (You might even want to have the article on hand to give him if he hasn't read it, but be prepared never to see it again, and don't expect him ever to sit down and read it. If you talk about it again, let it be at the professor's instigation. Let's face it, you are only making an impression—you must not ask for miracles.)

If you have nothing pressing that you have to say to the professor, then you have to find a way to say something useful, intelligent, or relevant. You must start to see this personal contact with the professor as one of your most important assignments in any course. At least as much depends upon the impression that you make on the professor outside of the class as the work you do in the class. If you show the professor that you have initiative, that you are making an effort, or that you have a particular interest in that subject, then the professor will take that impression to the grading of all your work, and it will affect your grade.

By the time your professor responds to one of your brief and specific questions, you will have a pretty good sense of whether she does, in fact, have a few minutes to spend with you or whether you should ingratiate yourself to her further by retreating as quickly as possible. Indeed, if your professor does not want to talk to you or simply cannot talk to you at that moment, she will be very grateful for your willingness to acknowledge this and leave her alone. It is probably a good idea, even after an interview with a professor begins, to offer to excuse yourself at each natural pause in the conversation. That will give you a sense of whether she wants you there or not. Also, watch the body language. If a professor does not sit down, does not offer you a seat, or stands up in the middle of the interview, then she probably wants the interview to end, and you can only score points by getting out.

LEND ME YOUR EARS

In the opposite scenario, the professor will have plenty of time, either because you happen to have caught him during a free moment or because he's simply bored or lonely and looking to kill some time. You will be able to recognize this professor immediately, either by the interest he shows in you upon your approach or by the air of desperation in his tone. This type of professor might greet you with a friendly entreaty to enter and have a seat in the office, or with a question like "How are things going with your work?" If he asks a general probing question to start the meeting, then you're in, and you'd better be up to one of your more impressive performances.

Despite this type of welcoming manner, it is probably better to let this professor lead you through the conversation, so look for a way to hand the conversation back to him as quickly as possible. Since you can never know what is on the professor's mind at any given moment, you do not want to take the unnecessary chance of saying something offensive. Chances are that if a professor happens to be bored and looking for a distraction, he'll also probably want to do all the talking during the discussion. Professors are an endless source of fascination to themselves, if to no one else. If your instructor fits this description, sit back and enjoy the ride.

Some professors, particularly the wackier ones, can be great entertainment, and the more you show that you are actually entertained by their musings, the more you will ingratiate yourself with them. (Whether you are entertained or not, try to appear so by articulating the occasional "oh" and "ah," if that is the effect that the professor is going for.) If the professor rambles on indefinitely about nothing in particular, then you must still nod appreciatively throughout the monologue, pretending to be interested. Most professors have bored generation after generation of students, and now it's your turn. They know they have a captive audience (usually, no one else listens to them—not their spouses or kids or friends or second cousins), so get comfortable.

Whatever you do, never show that you are bored or that you want to leave before the interview has ended. The longer that you sit nodding before the professor, the more familiar you will be to that person. If he's rambling on indefinitely, it just means that you have to do less of the work to sustain this growing familiarity between you and that person. Never try to excuse yourself while the professor is talking. Always, in these instances, wait to be excused. The time you have sacrificed in these seemingly interminable instances is time well invested.

If this professor begins asking questions that suggest that his primary interest is you and your life, then so much the better. However, you should try to maintain a respectful distance until the professor attempts to bridge that distance. Do not reveal anything that can be construed as overly personal or potentially embarrassing—you do not wish to alienate the professor by crossing any boundaries. For example, if the professor asks you whether you are enjoying your other courses, do not begin to speak insultingly about other professors unless this individual seems to want you to. If the professor asks about your personal life (family, relationships, and so on), do not reveal any personal problems unless, again, this individual seems to want to hear such revelations. Many professors will want to use you as a source of gossip for the little scandals that go on around every department. By all means, fuel the fire; if they want the information, tell them who is sleeping with whom, but always save some news for the next meeting—always keep them wanting more.

TREADING DANGEROUS WATERS

It is possible in these instances to test the waters. If, for example, a professor asks you how your other courses are going, you can say that you are not happy with some other course. If the professor wants the dirt on one of his colleagues, you can be certain that he'll push the conversation further. Professors who have been confined to the same department for a sufficient number of years tend to become bored and petty. They will often want to involve you in some sort of conspiracy against one of their colleagues, which is probably based on a rivalry or hostility that existed before you were born and will persist long after you leave. When this happens, you have the opportunity to develop a level of intimacy with the professor that will be unequaled by your fellow students. Of course, if the professor fails to push the issue of your problems with another professor further, then you can be certain that he would rather know no more.

The same holds true for developing an intimate dialogue with the professor about some particularly annoying student in your class who, it seems, is also annoying the professor. You can allude to the issue, you can subtly attempt to draw the professor out on that issue, but if the professor is wary and doesn't bite, then back off. If, during a lecture, an annoying student won't let the professor get through a point, you can later say, "It would have been nice to hear your whole lecture." If the professor jumps at this and complains bitterly about the student, then you're in—if the professor simply nods, then you have still scored a good point, but there is no reason to push it further.

Likewise, if a professor is interested in your personal life, the conversation will probably start out with some question like "So how was your Christmas vacation? Did you get to see your family?" or "Did you have a good time on the weekend?" If indeed there is a problem in your life that you think is relevant to your performance in the course, then you might say, "No, things haven't been going too well." Again, if the professor wants the topic to proceed any further at this point, then she will take the initiative and push it further. Don't hesitate to tell your professor if a problem is interfering with your performance in the course. You should simply be sensitive to the fact that the professor may not want to hear the details.

The worst thing that a student can do in approaching the professor out of class is to treat her like a personal psychiatrist. For some reason, this is more common than you would think.

Perhaps it is because professors seem nice in class, or perhaps some students simply know nobody else who they think would be insightful enough to understand their problem. Some small minority of professors do want to hear about your problems, and you can be sure that these individuals will draw it out of you in a very obvious way. Otherwise, do whatever you can to avoid talking about your personal problems because professors probably will not know how to deal with the situation, and their own ineptitude is disconcerting to them. The discomfort produced at this moment will make them uncomfortable with you in future dealings.

Even if you are approaching the professor for an extension on an assignment, and you need that extension because of some personal problem or another, then in your request, you should refer to that personal problem, only in the most general of terms. Under most circumstances, the professor will not want to know.

HARRY: I can recall one mature student who, whenever she engaged me in one-on-one conversations, would describe in detail how her performance in the course was affected by her current state of menopausal hell. Or her children's spouses' hemorrhoids. Or her father's multiple escapes from ''the home.'' Or (I am not making any of this up) some growth or another that had taken root on the skin surfaces of her various family members. As a result, she would inevitably, though not at all intentionally, send me fleeing for my life in any direction leading away from her.

Of course, I wanted to be sensitive. My intention was not to deny the trauma of her experience. I just didn't want to hear about it. I have no training in these areas, and such confidences are way more than I need to know. But because this was the pattern she established, I sought to avoid more confessions and revelations and ended up ducking out when I saw her winding her way to my office.

In such situations, you would be much better off simply commenting on the course, or asking where to find further reading on one of the subjects discussed in class and then informing your professor, in general terms, about certain health and personal problems that are keeping you from getting your work in on time. You might even ask for advice concerning whom to speak to about some personal difficulties. The question and its implications would be registered by the professor, the necessary extensions or special considerations granted, and the issue closed. The lasting effect of this kind of approach will be much more favorable—your professor will remember the difficulties you've been having and be more sympathetically inclined when it comes time to evaluate your performance.

STRIKING THE RIGHT NOTE

If the professor in question is one who appears to want the interview to end as quickly as possible, then you should maintain a serious and businesslike tone throughout the meeting. Never take the discussion in directions in which it seems the professor does not want to go and, again, always show that you are ready to leave as soon as the pressing issue is resolved. If, on the other hand, the professor seems to be interested in hearing more about you as a person, you might eventually, and very slowly, start to test the waters with a more personal tone. But you must always gauge the professor's response carefully. (Remember that, even at the most intimate level, the professor is *not* your friend, and that your relationship to this person means that you are always being evaluated in some way—so you are always working this person toward a specific end, a higher regard for you.)

You might begin this effort to become personal with some very neutral topic, such as "I guess we both know how difficult these late afternoon classes can be" or "You really seemed to be enthusiastic about that topic." If the professor, at this point, starts to open up personally, then she might eventually invite you to start sharing your personal responses as well. Once again, the important thing to remember is not to take any chances; you must always wait to be invited to share your feelings, or you could put yourself in danger of alienating the professor.

The possibility of bringing humor into the interview with the professor is the trickiest issue of all. There is nothing worse than

trying to invite the professor to share a laugh and failing miserably. You might discover one of two things: that the professor has
no sense of humor, or that you have no sense of delivery. You
might have to live through the awkward silence produced when
you find yourself dealing with an individual who initially appeared to have a good sense of humor but is, in fact, clued out
when it comes to the nuances of a good joke. Or, you might think
that you are capable of telling a good joke, but you may not know
that you have no comic timing at all and that your friends have
just not gotten around to telling you the bad news. Be very careful
in this area. Be certain that the joke or humorous comment is in
context and will work before you attempt it. If you fail in your
effort to introduce humor, once again you will alienate the professor, and you will be very hesitant to approach the professor in
the future.

If one of your jokes scores well, then you have made great
advances in your attempt to achieve a sympathetic relationship
with the professor. But never tell a joke that is off-color or racy
in any way. You do not know the professor's personal or political
position, and you never want to take the chance of offending.

THE EGO STROKE

The ego stroke is yet another opportunity to make great strides
(if you can do it properly and subtly). But, as with trying to tell
a joke to a professor, if you attempt the ego stroke and fail, you
will have failed quite miserably, and you might ruin your chances
of approaching that professor successfully at any time in the
future.

The ego stroke basically defines itself. A professor's self-per-
ception is guided primarily by intellect. He *is* his intellect, in the
same way that a rump roast will imply a butcher's worth in the
world. But professors can be vain in other ways as well. They can
see themselves as athletic, as sexy, as funny, as talented artists, as
snappy and fashionable dressers, and in a number of different
ways. The thing that you have to understand about these people
is that they are trapped in a very closed setting year after year,
and you are often the only new person who is going to come

along and confirm for them that they are really as great as they believe or hope themselves to be.

If you are clever, you can pick up on the image that the professor is trying to project, and flatter that professor in subtle ways. If the professor seems to be trying to be dapper, subtly compliment him on his clothes. Don't say something like, "Hey, I really like the way you dress," when you can say, "Where did you get that shirt? I'd like to get something like that for myself." (Don't forget that professors are always hoping to be accepted as belonging in this world that is perennially younger than they are—so don't say, "I'd like to get something like that . . . for my parents.") Don't say, "Boy, you are so funny" (nobody would fall for anything so obviously sycophantic), when you could as easily say, "It is so much easier to understand the material when it's delivered with some humor."

You can probably even stroke your professor's ego by suggesting that he doesn't look old enough to be a professor, or to have been a professor for as long as he has, or to have written as many published works as he has. You get the picture. If you see him in a hallway with his baby and you say, "Baby!? I thought that was your brother," you might be taking it a little too far. Make the professor feel attractive. You might even want to find a way, somehow, very carefully, to let the professor know that he is too attractive to be a professor, because chances are his colleagues haven't been winning any beauty pageants lately.

HARRY: You must always be careful in these instances, of course. I recall one young student telling me, during a chance meeting after class, that she did not feel that I was "the professor type," which was a fine and welcome statement for me personally because I understood it as a suggestion that I wasn't stuffy and out of touch. But some less-secure professors (and let me tell you they are abundant) might take it as a slight to their status and their attempt to establish themselves in the intellectual environment. Most professors want to be considered the intelligent type (though not so intelligent that they are thought the out-of-touch type, and not so in touch that they are perceived as superficial or ''lightweight,'' and yet not such a heavyweight that they are considered aloof and uncaring toward their students—whew!).

You see here how difficult the ego stroke is; you can see also how the professor will work and rationalize to take what you say as a compliment. You have to work hard to figure out what "type" your professor wants to be perceived as. Find her weakness, find her source of vanity—exploit it for all it's worth.

Ultimately, there is no ego stroke for a professor like the intellectual ego stroke. Your professors earn their living by their mind alone, so they will want to be told that you consider their mind to be of the top caliber, that their classes are the most stimulating, that you have sought out their publications (always try to be familiar with their work outside the classroom) and found them eye opening. Most importantly, you should, if the opportunity arises, stroke your professor's ego not only by praising her work, but by trying to give her the sense that her work is that much more important, and that her classes are that much more interesting, than her colleagues'.

Again, this must be handled very carefully. Don't name names when placing your professor's work over that of her colleagues. Simply suggest that you are taking other classes, and that you are familiar with the work of other professors, and that, based upon your own experience, her work is the best that you have encountered. But be more specific than "best." Try something like, "I'm really interested in that idea of _____ that you were talking about in class. I haven't heard anything in any of my other classes that makes that much sense to me." Or "I had been thinking of switching disciplines until I took your class, but now the theories are finally becoming a lot clearer. Where do you think I should take my studies from here? Are you teaching any other classes along the same lines?"

Basically, what the ego stroke comes down to is this: if you are talking to someone who sells shirts, you compliment the shirts he makes because that is what he does; if you are talking to someone who paints landscapes, you compliment her landscapes because that is what she does; it is the same with interior designers, architects, car mechanics, body builders, chefs, you name it—the identities of these people are locked up in what they do, so you make them feel good about themselves by complimenting the products that they make. Why should things be any different with professors? Their product is their intellect and their ideas, and if you compliment those ideas or the way the ideas are presented, then you are reaffirming everything that that person does and stands for. So find a way to do it!

CALL 1-900-ASK-PROF
(Slight penalty the first minute, heavy cost every minute thereafter.)

Calling a professor at home is a risky proposition. There is probably no way that the home phone call can work to improve your standing with the professor, or to develop a sympathetic relationship between you and the professor in the same way that the interview in the professor's office can advance your standing. The home phone call is to be used not as a strategy in advancing your relationship with the professor, but only when you need a response to a pressing matter that cannot wait. When you appear at the professor's office with a valid inquiry, you will be perceived as an enthusiastic student; when you call the professor at home, you are a pest—or worse.

There is no way around it. When you call your professor at home, you can be certain that you will be interrupting the season finale of "ER," or you will be jumping into the middle of a major blow-out fight with his or her spouse (or, much worse, you will be interrupting their making-up session after the fight)—either way, your call will not be welcome.

As a general rule, never call a professor at home unless he has given out his phone number in class and provided specific guidelines under which the call can be made. A colleague of ours outlined a rule for students to follow if they absolutely had to call her at home: "Never call and ask, 'Is it too late to be calling you?' If it is late enough for you to imagine even asking that question, then rest assured that it is too late to be calling me at home." One student of ours called after midnight on several successive nights to explain why her essay was late, and later, and later still. When her assignment finally showed up, the presumptuousness of her behavior couldn't help but find its way into the reception of the paper and register in her grade. In many cases, your professors will have young children who may be napping at any hour of the day—wake the kid and you're doomed forever. Common sense should guide you in these instances.

WHAT'S A NICE PROF LIKE YOU DOING IN A PLACE LIKE THIS?

And then there are those potentially embarrassing moments when you see your professor out on the town, or in a restaurant, or in a parking lot, or at the supermarket, or in a magazine store shopping for porn. Neither of you will quite know how to react in these situations. And, to make matters worse, you really don't know whether your professor has any idea who you are. So there you are, fearing that if you approach him you might make a fool of yourself, and if you don't approach him you might offend him because he might be expecting you to acknowledge him. He may even be out on the town with friends, hoping you will come by to say "hi" so that his friends can see how well-liked and approachable he is. If he has identified you to his friends as one of his students, and then you snub him, the public humiliation he might feel at this will be channeled into a negative impression of you, which will trickle down until it spills out on the grade sheet.

The truth is that the accidental meeting outside of the university setting, unlike the home phone call, can only work to your advantage. First of all, you must approach, even if you feel as though you will be making a fool of yourself by doing so. Always say at least a pleasant, if quick, "hello" to your professors when you see them away from their usual setting. At best, the professor will actually know you and be happy, or at least not *un*happy, that you bothered to pay your respects.

But what if the professor has no idea who you are? While this seems like a very uncomfortable proposition, there is, in fact, no better way to build a type of familiarity with a professor who might otherwise have never noticed you at all. If the professor does not know who you are under these conditions, then rest assured that the embarrassment belongs to him, not you. At worst, you will recognize the lack of recognition, and you can seize the opportunity to introduce yourself. But, of course, you must be polite and gracious; after introducing yourself, prove your own benevolence with a statement like "Well, you have so many students, how could you possibly remember every last one." The professor will be eternally grateful for your efforts to save his face. Thereafter, he will never dare forget you. There will be instant recognition in the next class, and from that point forth—maybe you can even begin your next dialogue with a reference to that previous chance meeting (unless it occurred at the local strip club).

As with all other encounters with your professors, you should never let the accidental meeting drag on, unless it is the professor who demands that you continue to interact with her. But you can be more familiar in a neutral setting; if you see the professor in a bar or a supermarket or anywhere else away from the university, you have free reign to let her know that you are now aware of her status as something other than only a professor. Don't push it too far—don't follow her around the supermarket commenting on each product she buys, reminding her that fat-free products are healthier and that Wisk is on sale this week at a lower price than her brand of stain remover.

In the accidental encounter, it is the setting that will humanize you both and advance your relationship from a strictly professional level to something more ordinary, more familiar. You should never miss the opportunity to advance your relationship with a professor this extra step when fate draws you together in the real world and gives you the opening on a silver platter. You can always start out with something as friendly and as harmless as, "So, you guys *do* have a life outside of the classroom." Nobody, not even the stuffiest ones, could possibly take offense to this.

THE COCKTAIL HOUR

Finally, there are those occasions in every student's university career where you find yourself, after a class or after the last class of the term, at a campus bar, enjoying a celebratory beer with your professor. This, in theory, should be an ideal opportunity to advance your standing in the professor's mind. Why else bother? It's not as though this professor could possibly be better company than your own friends.

But the after-class beer is usually more of a mirage in the

desert of growing familiarity with the professor. From our experiences both as students and as professors, these situations are never anything other than uncomfortable and stale. No one seems to know if these meetings are an extension of the class or something else that would be impossible to define. No one knows quite what to say, and everyone simply ends up sitting around, staring at one another, saying only the dumbest things, which are supposed to sound casual or funny, like, "Hey, how 'bout that discussion of B. F. Skinner? Was that something?" or "Did you get to watch any of the football play-offs? No? Oh, that's too bad. Ya, it was neat."

Everyone ends up vying for little moments of the professor's attention, and the professor ends up watching the clock, praying for the seconds to tick by a little more quickly until she feels she has made an appearance of proper length. The gathering, organized by whomever with only the best intentions, is never pleasant, never casual, and never effective in advancing your standing in the professor's mind. (Unless it is the professor who has initiated the gathering so that she can hold court for a couple of hours—in this case, do your best to pretend that you find her endless droning amusing.)

Our general advice on the after-class beer is to stay away if you can do so politely. At least, never be the person to instigate this small celebration because it won't be remembered or appreciated by your professor. If you must go, then sit as far as possible from her at the table. That way it will register with the professor that you were actually there, but you will not be associated, in her mind, with the excruciating quality of the evening.

BEGGING TO DIFFER

Of course, ultimately there is only one reason why you would put yourself through the trial of interacting with your professor outside the classroom—you want her to know you well enough that she will almost be forced to give you a good grade, whether you have earned it or not. This leads us, once and for all, to the most important visit that you will ever make to your professor's office— that in which you beg a better grade than the one you received. Not only is this the most important visit, but it is the most sensitive and potentially the most volatile as well. All students who have aspired to use their university grades to catapult them to success have attempted the big beg at some point in their university career, though probably only a small minority of these students have pulled it off successfully. That is because few students can anticipate what is going on in their professor's mind while they build their argument. When it comes to the big beg, there are many statements that are guaranteed to fail, and only a few that might succeed.

Certain statements associated with the big beg seem like logical things to say, but are guaranteed to piss your professor off royally. If you blurt out any of these major blunders, you can be sure that your professor will not only refuse your appeal, but will be gunning to challenge you again and again in the future with even lower grades. The worst, and most common, of these blunders is the seemingly innocent statement "But I get good grades in all my other courses."

Now, what you are trying to express with this statement is something like, "I have been doing well in my other courses, and I am very worried that this one grade might hurt my standing. The only measure that I have to gauge my progress is my other grades." (A fair sentiment, indeed, and in some cases it might even be true.) However, your professor's first thought when you present this innocent argument will be something like, "You are so full of shit!" Then, your professor's next series of thoughts will be, "Are you trying to tell me that there is something wrong with me because I don't know as much as all my colleagues? Are you trying to tell me that I don't know what I'm doing because I can't recognize your genius? Well, let me tell you something, punk, if you're gonna challenge my authority, then let's see how you handle even lower grades in your other assignments. You want a fight—you've got a fight."

You see, the professor is an insecure animal, and the last thing he wants is to feel that he is being compared unfavorably to his colleagues, who he no doubt hates. The only thing that has gotten him through the day is the feeling that he's actually superior to the professor in the next office. The last thing that he wants to hear is that students are starting to favor the jerk next door over him. Such is your professor's ego and insecurity. Pathetic—but it's better that you find out now.

So how is the big beg done right? There is only one sure-fire method. Rather than arguing that you deserve a better grade because your other grades are higher, you must articulate your argument based upon your feelings about your own personal best. Rather than saying, "My other grades are better," you should say something like, "I know that I am capable of better, and I just wanted to ask what I have to do to start getting grades at the A level because I really have to do better to get into this graduate course in accounting/human resources/comparative literature/nursing/[whatever]." Once you say this, the professor will know that you are challenging yourself, not him, and he'll be looking for ways of getting you to the level that you have expressed as your desired goal. Also, when a professor is made to articulate clearly to you the qualities of excellent work, then he becomes involved in your aspiration—now the two of you are working together toward an end, and he becomes mixed up in your success or, now unlikely, failure.

SUMMING UP

Perhaps the best rules to remember when schmoozing your professor is that she wants to be made to feel important, but at the same time she doesn't want to be pestered. She wants to be made to feel significant without having to work very hard. She wants to be made to feel superior to her colleagues without having to publish quite as much or without having to be quite as interesting. She wants to feel worshiped for her intellect without feeling as though you are actively, obviously worshiping. She does not want to be made to feel like the dinosaur that she is, even though you, like the students who have appeared in these classrooms before you and those students yet to come, are better looking, are in better shape, are in better touch with the real world, have greater prospects. Nor does she want to be reminded that you are having better sex than she is.

Make her feel like she is impressive to you, and then quickly withdraw. Make her feel like her work is helping in your growth, and then quickly withdraw. Make her feel needed. Make her feel intelligent. Make her feel superior and lofty, and then leave her alone to remember your name and the way you made her feel.

CHAPTER 5

* * *

Essays and Exams

HOW TO SHOW YOU CARE WHEN
YOU CAN'T BE THERE

Okay, so we've told you a few things about how to play the various interpersonal aspects of the professor-student relationship, but what about the real meat of the university system—essays and examinations? No matter how well you play the game in the classroom, no matter how smooth you are in the office and hallway and hardware store encounters, you are eventually going to have to hand over some work—if you don't, where's the professor going to exercise her subjective control? The essay or the examination is the physical object on which the professor will express how well you've been playing the game: a piece of work that might, under neutral circumstances, land firmly in C land, will, if you've placed yourself in the inner circle, be bumped into the far happier and sunnier B land. So, for the most part, the assignments and examinations are really just the opportunity for the professor to reward, punish, or shrug. Yet, the physical objects themselves also can be finessed in certain ways so that, at the very moment of grading, you give your professor a gentle nudge that reminds her of her pleasant relationship with you.

But be advised: in isolation, the essay and examination strategies mentioned below are maneuvers that should be attempted only by students who have already, in those other political arenas, received signals that they have been playing the game well. If your professor has been responding to you, calling on you in class without her eyes rolling back in her head, smiling when you enter the classroom, or welcoming you into her office without sighing and reaching up to give her temples a pressured rub, then the techniques discussed in this chapter will only help to remind her of that relationship. But if you have not been getting signals that your relationship with the professor is a good one, or if you haven't been able to step out from the wallpaper, then any essay or examination tactic will not get the relationship working for you (and, in fact, if the move is seen as an attempt to suck up, it will only backfire). So use these recommendations in conjunction with, rather than as steps toward the development of, a good working relationship with your professor.

** WRITING ESSAYS **

FILL IN THE BLANK

At some time in your university career, regardless of your chosen field of study, you're going to find yourself staring at a blank page or a flashing cursor on an otherwise empty computer screen, trying to come up with a way to fill the page or screen that will prompt its eventual reader to dole out the sticky gold star. Now, we're sure you've written some essays in high school, and hey, you may even have been asked to read your essay on the subject of Neptune aloud to the entire Grade 11 science class. But the university essay is a different deal altogether. You can't imagine the number of first-year faces we've seen crumple up and start to quiver after getting their first university essay back. Now, as much as we enjoy that crushed look and get a real kick out of mimicking it at our faculty lounge Christmas parties, there are a number of things you can do to minimize the devastation.

The university essay requires research, a clear and mature sense of the process or logic of argument, grammatical sophistication, and a variety of other technical and intellectual qualities. But we have no intention of helping you with any of that. There are plenty of adequate books on these subjects, books designed to show you how to work harder and more effectively. You already know you can (should?) do this, but we promised our book would boost your grades without demanding this kind of work.

Once again, we want to show you the process as it is seen from the cluttered side of the professor's desk. Few professors will include essay grading in their list of "a few of my favorite things." Essay grading is the slog work of the job. It has none of the fun of performance (lectures), and it is quite literally thankless (well, okay, somewhere along the line a student might thank his professor for giving him an academic wake-up call, but most of the time, the professor can look forward to nothing but disappointed faces and accusing glares). Essay grading is also the most time-consuming of the professor's teaching tasks: the average essay (say, 8 to 12 pages) takes 45 minutes to an hour to grade. Multiply this by the average class size, and then again by the professor's course load, and you can understand why the prospect might get instructors down—particularly given the reactions they can look forward to once the papers are given back. So if you, as a student, can make this process in any way easier or faster, your professor will be grateful, and that gratitude will be expressed in the slight inflation of your grade.

The first thing you should know is that it is way easier to grade a good paper than it is to grade a bad one (well, of course, that depends on how bad, but we're talking about the average C or D paper here). A bad paper requires much more effort; the professor has to pay more attention to correcting, and each sentence slows her down as she works to try to decipher the gist of the thing and to reveal to the student where to improve and what has gone wrong. The bad paper is also frustrating for the professor because she wants you to get it. She is teaching the course to enlighten and inform, and a bad paper tells her that either you are not paying attention or she's not teaching properly (and she'll almost always choose to believe the former). So the good paper has two things going for it: it's good, and it's a quick and refreshing stop for the professor on the long route through the pile of term papers to the surface of her desk. So even if you can't write a good paper, making your paper easier to get through by doing simple things like running a spell check, proofreading, and avoiding careless errors will make a huge difference to the profes-

sor and make the paper come off as less bad than it might otherwise seem.

SETTING THE MOOD

The suggestions offered in this section will get you higher grades,
but they will only operate to their full potential if you have already
established a positive relationship with your professor, as de-
scribed in previous chapters. If your essay is plunked down in
front of the professor, and he has no face or history to associate
with it, then the techniques explored here won't carry the same
kind of power. To maximize the grade growth, you need to prepare the ground for this seed.

Over the last three yeas at the grading desk, we've been noticing a trend. It's nothing we've done consciously, but it is something we've become aware of. While working away grading
papers, we'll come to one by a student whose name is unfamiliar.
For a brief but glorious moment, we'll hope that the paper got
into our mailboxes by mistake, but after finding the name on the
class list, we'll settle down to grade it. While working through the
paper, adding comments and little check marks, all we're thinking
about is a range of numbers. But, with students who have made
themselves known to us, students who, for some of the reasons
discussed in the other chapters, have become comforting and familiar, accompanying that range of numbers is an image of that
person's face—a face that reacts with each comment written and
each check mark ticked off. When faced with a human and reactive
presence like that, it becomes difficult to be harsh.

DAVID: If I like a particular student, then I have a more difficult time doing something I know will make her unhappy. On
the other hand, the paper from the student whose name I don't
recognize, the paper that has me thinking exclusively of a
range of numbers, gives me no incentive to be more inclined
toward the higher end of that range. If I'm thinking the paper
could likely receive anything between a 72 and a 76 percent,
the number I pick will likely have to do with my mood and the
number I gave to this student's last paper.

Remember what we said in the second chapter about feeling that pressure to produce a range of grades? That pressure means we look for papers to bring down the average, and it's easier to give that average-lowering grade to a student with whom we have not established a friendly relationship.

If the truth be told (and we told you we'd tell it), the paper by the familiar and comforting student is probably already working within a higher range of numbers than the one by the faceless student. We are absolutely certain that if two papers were submitted to the same professor, and these papers were identical except that one was written by an unknown student and the other by a known and liked student, they would receive distinctly different grades—and we have no doubt that the known and liked student would be the one with the better transcript for his application to graduate or professional schools.

Now, please don't take this as a recommendation to print a photograph of your face on the title page of your essays. The essay should arrive on the professor's desk (or in the professor's hands) with the groundwork already firmly laid. The development of a positive history with the professor will go much further than any tricks of essay presentation toward gaining you the position of advantage, but this said, there are things you can do in and around the essay itself that will help in the process.

TRICKS OF THE PAPER TRADE

The first and simplest trick is not really a trick: write an absolutely fabulous first paper. If you blow your professor away with your very first effort, and she puts you up there in that comfortable A range, then it becomes very difficult for her to bring you back down on subsequent essays. Not only does bringing your next grade down mess up her sense of typical progress, but the first essay will predispose your professor to believe that your work is of a different quality, and she will work to see again the glimmer of previous shinings. She'll expect the best, and so she's more apt to see the paper that way. But, then, it is no great secret that you should always write as strong an essay as you are capable. So, when it comes to the essay paper, what can you do above and beyond this?

FABLES OF CONTENT

In terms of content, many students believe that professors simply want a regurgitation of their ideas or lectures. This assumption is false . . . and true. It is false in the sense that professors want the student to show some signs of processing the information given in lectures. Blow fluid rather than chunks. Professors want students to be able to express the ideas in their own way, and likely will demand that students explore the idea in more detail than might have been possible in a lecture covering a whole range of topics or applications. So a simple repetition of the material as covered will likely not impress the professor.

Yet, there is much to be said for confirming your professors' notions and opinions. Your professors usually will make their positions on issues and topics known to the class. If the contents of your essay affirm through argument and analytical process an idea that you know the professor supports, then the inclination on the part of the professor will be to overlook (or not weigh so heavily) minor weaknesses. These minor weaknesses, in a paper that took a position opposing that held by the professor, might be made to count for more by that professor, who has an interest in defending his position. Simply stated, if you agree with the professor he'll likely find the paper more agreeable, and the same goes for disagreement.

Don't be a weenie! Or, at least, don't be perceived as being a weenie. By all means listen to the lectures and incorporate the ideas surfacing here—but do so in your own distinct fashion. If you are going to borrow the professor's language or phrasings, be absolutely sure that you use them correctly. Along similar lines, never use overly elevated vocabulary, particularly if it is elevated so much that it is over your own head. One of us has always had a particular interest in a thing called the panopticon (it's sort of a prison model designed by an eighteenth-century philosopher). So this term often came up in some way in classes. One student decided that this obvious interest was reason enough to pepper his paper with the word *panopticon* with no regard to its suitability. This kind of thing is an obvious attempt to gain favor, and it ends up failing miserably (as did the student) because you've approached an area that you know your professor is interested in, but you've only drawn attention to your lack of competence in that area. If you are genuinely interested in an obvious pet project of your professor, then the best thing to do is seek him out for private counsel and clarification (more on this private consult later).

We don't want you to think we're advising you to always agree with your professors in your essays. We're not (we probably should, but our consciences won't let us get away with it). Put it this way: by all means challenge your professor's positions, but to do so, your relationship with him must be strong, and you must be prepared to do twice as good a job to get the same grade as you might have for a paper agreeing with him.

A colleague of ours teaches Shakespeare's *Tempest*, and every year he goes about the task of tearing down the main character, Prospero, who, our friend argues, is a racist politician who manipulates women and the natural world to serve his own ends. Yet, nonetheless, each year, he receives about four essays that seemingly ignore his lectures and defend Prospero as a heroic man who saves the island and brings everything to a happy ending. These essays get, what we in the business call, the slam dunk. Imagine the sound your paper would make as it hit the garbage can at one hundred miles per hour—that's what the professor is imagining with the slam dunk. When this colleague was asked whether it was possible for a student to write a pro-Prospero paper and still prosper, our colleague grudgingly admitted that such a paper would have to be an incredibly tight piece of analysis that took into account many of his objections because otherwise he would have to believe that this evidence was being intentionally overlooked for the sake of a clean argument. In other words, it is possible, but not bloody likely.

CONSPIRACY TO COMMIT TO PAPER

An important issue in all of this concerns the extent to which you should involve your professor in the process of your essay writing. Involving the professor, by seeking her advice, by getting clarification of the question, and by other means, can, if handled in the correct manner, turn the professor into a kind of co-conspirator. The visited professor has invested time and energy in you and tried to help you with ideas and strategies for the paper, so when those ideas and strategies show up, she knows that she has to take at least partial responsibility. But, as with the office visit in general, this approach needs to be handled carefully; this kind of contact can produce a powerful ally or a determined enemy.

First, never approach your professor with a basic question about your essay within the two-week period before it is due. The reason for this should be obvious. A basic question like "I wondered if we could go over a couple of the essay topics because I'm having trouble deciding" tips her off that you haven't started the paper yet. This will likely offend her sense of the importance the thing should have for you. Never let the professor know how much time you have allotted to the writing of an essay paper. If she knows you wrote it only a couple of days before, or, worse yet, the night before, then that knowledge will prompt her to look for signs of haste and sloppiness.

This two-week boundary applies to initial and general questions only, questions like the one above about discussing and clarifying essay topics. Once you have broken the ice on the essay with the professor, follow-up questions can come anywhere within the period approaching the deadline. But don't phone the professor the night before—even if you are asking for more time. The night-before phone call to the home is an invasion, an irritation, and it signals to the professor nothing except that you are unprepared, unorganized, and in way over your head—a signal that the professor will remember when she sits down to grade your paper (when it eventually shows up).

But getting help from the professor on a paper is a crucial step in securing the success of the paper. As we mentioned in the chapter on the office visit, arrive for help with very specific questions, not just vague expressions of difficulty. Asking for clarification of a question or asking about particular strategies of approach to a question gets the professor to start talking about the way in which he might approach the issue. And this gets you that much closer to an understanding of his sense of the ideal answer. You might even bring in a question based on information you got in lectures, and the office setting will allow the professor to flesh out his opinions. A question like "My paper is on the editorial in journalism: doesn't all journalistic writing have that opinionated editorial quality in some way?" will allow the professor to take you by the hand and lead you right into the kind of material that will be "right" for your essay. So get him involved by seeking him out in office hours and asking very focused questions—even questions about library resources or proper format. A question like "If I'm to compare and contrast Marx with Lenin, should each paragraph consider both guys, or should I separate them into sections?" will make the professor contribute to the paper in a way that he will have to recognize when he comes to grade it. And when he sees himself in your essay, he'll fall in love with that image.

DO YOU FEEL A DRAFT?

We've had students show up in our offices with a draft of their paper in their hand, hoping that we'll go over it with them. Some professors just won't do this, but we've never been against it, as long as the student presents the sense of the draft orally rather than just asking us to read it and tell them if it's okay. Showing your professors a draft, or telling them about your draft, can get you bonus grades—the professor sees diligence, sees that you've allowed sufficient time to work and rework, and sees that you are committed enough to the course to be this concerned about your direction and product. But feel the professor out. Ask her first if this would be okay with her, and, if so, approach her with very focused questions rather than just "Could you look this over?" You can talk about the structure of the paper, its logic; you might even give her the gist of your first paragraph (the one that introduces your argument) and ask her if this opening has what it takes to set up a successful paper.

Here's the crucial thing though: if you are going to do the draft show, then be prepared for criticisms and be prepared to rework your paper to address those criticisms. We've had students bring drafts to us that we've found a number of problems with, and yet their final papers were handed in with virtually the same text as the draft. If you don't really want the advice, and aren't willing to change the paper, then don't do the draft show—any bonus grades you might have gained by your show of diligence and concern will be lost twice over when the professor realizes with the final product that you were only doing it for show.

THE HAND-OFF

Two things: put the essay on the professor's desk or in her hand and then go away. Don't feel that you must deliver an elaborate prologue when you hand over your essay for grading. If the essay is on time (which it should be), and you're handing it in with everyone else in the class (which you should be), then simply add it to the pile and move on down the hall.

Some students believe a little modesty or self-deprecation is in order at the hand-off: "Well, here it is. I'm really disappointed with it, but I gave it a shot." The strategy here employs the same thinking as fishing for a compliment. Someone says, "My hair's a disaster today," wanting the listener to deny it ("Oh no, hey, you look fabulous!"). But think about this: often the responder is just saying this because she feels it is socially required—she probably does think your hair is a disaster today. Also remember that professors have no basic social training—they don't have to live in society. (If you don't believe us, watch for the next academic conference hosted by your university, and go to the cocktail party— they have all the style of your parents dancing to Pearl Jam.) So the introductory gesture of modesty is not going to work for you; it is more likely to work against you and make your professor expect (and find) a poor result.

The same principle applies to the overconfident approach: "Man, this essay is gonna blow your mind!" A statement like this is likely to be received by professors as a challenge. Remember, they have a stake in the control of this subject, and if you tell them that you've nailed it, they're going to show you where you're wrong. So the best strategy here is a short hand-off: let the quarterback call the play.

Finally, don't be that student—there's one every time an essay is submitted—who asks, "Hey, you got a stapler?" (What am I, the Office Depot? Don't make me come over there!)

THAT'S NOT FUNNY

Though most professors have relaxed the rules over the years, generally speaking, the essay is understood to be a formal occasion. That doesn't mean that it has to be as stiff as a three-day-dead lizard, but it does mean that there will be expectations concerning the tone of your writing. One of our student's essays was entitled "Dissing the Sixteenth Century." We were (are?) still young enough to know what this meant and think it funny, but we know that some of our colleagues, they of the well-worn elbow patches, would simply think that it was a typo for "Missing the Sixteenth Century" and think that's exactly what the student had done—missed it. When it comes to humor and colloquialisms (informal or slang words), less is more. A well-timed joke or break of form can be a refreshing change of pace for a grader and can positively dispose him toward the paper. But once per paper is enough, and even then, only if you have a history with the professor that makes you certain that the attempt will be well received.

PACKAGING

Your essay should be generated on a computer printer or typed. In California, where they have the time and inclination to do such things, a study was conducted among university faculty that compared the grades given to student papers that were identical except for the fact that one version was handwritten and the other was typed. The typed version was given an average grade that was 7 percent higher than that of its handwritten counterpart. And it's not just California that's superficial; the physical presentation of your essay at universities from coast to coast will have an impact on your grade. Now, you're going to pass a course on the basis of your typing alone (we're not talking about a typing course here), but, on the other hand, a well-typed paper will not lose grades for poor presentation.

The physical presentation of the paper matters for a couple of very simple reasons. We've told you that as far as professors go, the path of least resistance is generally the best—if you make things easier for them, you will be rewarded. A typewritten essay is easier to read. It also looks more professional, looks like it was produced with more care, and looks finished.

DAVID: I've been handed essays that stunk of cigarette smoke and cat pee, that were crumpled up, ringed with coffee stains, and, once, even one that was partially incinerated. Essay papers like this only give the professor a glorious set-up: to the student whose paper smelled of cat pee, I wanted to write, ''I have nothing to add that the cat hasn't already said.''

A recent study proved that "good-looking" people get along easier in life and are generally more successful. The same is true of essay papers: a well-groomed, clean copy will go farther. This may sound petty and prickly, but, to the professor, the physical artifact of the essay represents your level of concern about the course, and if a professor thinks you don't care enough to send the very best, then you're not going to get their best (grades) either.

DRESSING UP

White paper, clear plain script, and a single metallic paper clip. That's all it takes; that's all the professor wants. Personal computers, while they have made editing and printing terrifically simple, have also made it easier for students to ornament their essays more lavishly than Christmas trees. In fact, one year, the title page of one student's midterm essay paper was a computer-generated image of Santa with a big bag of loot (and this printed on red paper to boot!). Perhaps the goal was to get her professor in the festive and giving spirit before grading. It didn't. Humbug! These kinds of enhancements to your essay go nowhere. They're distracting and obvious and inappropriate. And, to a very traditional professor, they might be understood to cheapen the sacred form of the academic essay.

Computers also make it easy for you to explore a variety of intricate and dazzling fonts. Let the ease with which this can be achieved be a warning to you. Though 𝒞𝓇𝒶𝓏𝒽𝑜𝓊𝓈𝑒 and **FRAZZLE** may look awesome to you, to professors who are slogging through their fourth essay in a twelve-essay night, your paper will look like a traffic accident that is going to jam them up for hours.

Along similar lines, don't submit your essays in fancy binders. While it might be amusing to imagine your professor sweating to bend the stupid thing back to read that word on the left-hand margin of page 3, the frustration the professor goes through in the process will almost certainly show up in the grade given to the paper. Binders are always in the way; if you feel you must protect the pristine integrity of your paper, use an open file folder and don't expect to see it ever again. Speaking confessionally, we have between us quite a substantial collection of confiscated colorful plastic-coated paper clips and jazzy file folders in the bottom drawer of our desks. They're great for making necklaces and airplanes when we're bored.

Simplicity is perfection. White paper, clear plain script, and a single metallic paper clip.

BUT WHO'S COUNTING

In terms of the essay and your professor, there are three crucial points of advice: 1) never make the same mistakes as the ones the professor pointed out on your first paper; 2) always stay within the page limit; and 3) use spell-check functions and don't misspell the names of the authors or titles you're writing about.

Though university professors have the reputation, thanks to Hollywood (and some truly nutty professors), for being absent-minded, there are some things that really stick in their memories. Repetition of error is one of those things. Remember, professors hate grading. It is time-consuming, soul killing, and thankless. When they spend time on your essays, lavishing comments and advice, they want to think that it means something to you, that they are instructing you, and that you are learning. So if you repeat those mistakes on your next papers, they see that as a sign that their initial investment of time and energy in you was wasted. They will resent you for ignoring their hard work. And there's nothing more dangerous than a resentful professor.

Another excellent way to foster resentment in your professor is to give her a thirteen-page essay when she asked for an eight-page one. You see, the professor doesn't really want you to think that anything as mundane as page counting goes on in her office. It is the room, after all, for higher thought. But one of the first things that we all do when we start marking a paper is flip ahead to the last page and see what we're up against. If that thing is even a page over the maximum suggested, we feel as if we've just encountered a four-mile detour on our way home. However, afraid of seeming petty and unwilling to confess that we're just pissed off because you made us read six more pages than we had to, we'll tell you that part of the exercise was confining your argument within the required range. And we'll say that your failure to master this writing skill had to be measured and figured into the final grade. Slam dunk!

VIRTUES OF OMISSION

For the essay, playing the game mostly means not doing stuff. Professors want to get through this grading process and on to things that are more fun, like dental hygiene or hemorrhoid therapy. Make the process easy for them and they'll reward you for it. Omit the fancy typefaces, the gold-leaf paper in the leatherette binder, and so on, and expend your time and effort in more efficient ways. The most important thing is to have this relationship working well before the essay or examination. But seeking advice from your professor in advance, taking that advice, and gently reminding him of the nature of your good relationship with him will all help that relationship produce its positive effect on your grade.

✻✻ WRITING EXAMS ✻✻

GRACE UNDER PRESSURE

The entire term has passed. Throughout the eight months of the school year, you have worked very hard and succeeded in creating a friendly, sympathetic relationship with your professors. You have spoken with them casually in their office, in the classroom, in the corridors, at the cafeteria, wherever you "happened" to run into them. You are confident that, because of these efforts, your professors know you and see you as a pleasant, intelligent, motivated student. So far over the course of the year, the grades that you have received on individual assignments have reinforced your belief that you have played the game right—you have established contact with your professors, and you have succeeded in receiving grades and comments that suggest that they know you as a human being and are sympathetic to your desire to succeed in the course.

But suddenly you are cast into an entirely different setting and an entirely different role. Instead of finding yourself in the comfortable classroom or the professor's familiar office surroundings, you arrive in a massive, overwhelming gymnasium with row after row of desks upon which are daunting, overturned exam booklets. Your professor is present, but she is not in a position to exchange ideas or to socialize—she too is in the process of playing out a role, which has changed from an instructive, talkative lecturer to a stern, silent supervisor scanning the room, looking like a cop with a hunch of some wrongdoing happening on her beat. (In other words, she knows that there are crib sheets out there somewhere, and dammit, it's her job to find them!) Though you and the professor recognize each other, it would seem that neither of you is the same person you have been all year—your identities have been altered by the new surroundings and situation.

In some respects, part of the examination lies outside the questions written on the exam sheet or what you write in the exam booklet; part of the examination will be in how you respond to the professor at this moment, and in how you manage, in this setting, to remind the professor that she has been impressed by you all year, that the two of you have established a relationship strong enough to carry over into the exam experience and the grade ultimately placed on the exam paper. If you have run this marathon like a champ all year, you don't want to lose your edge in the home stretch! This is where you have to reach back and make that extra effort.

Are you, at this moment, expected to greet the professor with the usual friendly "hello," or does this intensified moment call for another response altogether? Is the professor, at this moment, in fact the same person that you remember from the classroom, or has she been transformed, in this alien setting, into a completely different entity—the *enemy*? Are you allowed to speak with the professor once you have finished the exam, or does your association with each other effectively terminate the second that you have scribbled your final comments into the exam booklet or answer sheet? Most importantly, are there ways, during the two or three pressure-packed hours of the exam-writing experience, to continue "playing" the professor—to continue reminding her that there is still a personal relationship between the two of you, that you have a history together? In this dramatic context, can you remind the professor in a way that will ensure that she will take that personal experience into the grading of your exam?

In this section, you will be introduced to some of the "tricks" that you might use to make contact with the professor while writing the exam. Like all the other advice given in this book, these tricks must be used with great care and sensitivity, or they may end up backfiring.

TWO SIDES TO EVERY STORY

First, let's look at the exam experience from your professor's point of view. No matter how old, seasoned, or indifferent your professors appear to be, you can be certain that they, like you, enter the exam room full of nervousness and anxiety, though the reasons for their case of nerves are quite a bit different from your own. One of the reasons that they might be on edge is that, whether they are aware of it or not, they have grown to like some of their students over the course of the year, and they are concerned for the well-being of those students. They are afraid that they might have made some of the questions too hard or that they may not have taught certain sections well enough in class. When they see you, they may be feeling a certain amount of guilt or responsibility for the experience that you are about to go through. They probably know, somewhere in their subconscious, that exams are an inadequate or at least artificial way to test knowledge, and that you can display very little of what you have learned in such a short period of time. But they want to have made it as fair and as useful as possible.

The other reason they might be nervous at this moment is a little more selfish. Sure they might be feeling a little tickle of sympathy for you at the back of their brain, but more importantly they know that your performance on the exam will reflect back on them and on their ability to teach the course material effectively. Your failure is, to some extent, their failure as well. If you have established relationships with your professors over the year, by the time the exam rolls around they want you to do well, both because they are concerned about you and your chances for future success, and because their egos will suffer a severe blow if you fail to prove that they were right in investing their own sense of self-worth in your ability. Also, a professor will take a certain amount of pride in having "bright" students; the idea is that your brightness is somehow produced, nurtured, or developed by them, and this ultimately gives them bragging rights in the faculty lounge over those other professors lamenting their more dim-witted students.

On judgment day, when the professor is faced with a huge stack of exams to be graded, there's not really a whole lot of difference between papers. This is particularly true in the case of exams in the humanities and the social sciences. With the possible exception of the two or three weakest and the two or three strongest exams in the pile, they all look pretty much the same (particularly given the speed at which the professor is going to cruise through them). When students are asked to write everything they know in such a brief, pressure-filled sitting, the playing field will be leveled and most students will end up writing pretty much the same thing (or at least display a similar range of knowledge). There is no time to formulate carefully worded and thought-out arguments; basically, no matter how hard students try to rise above the situation, the best that most people can do is scramble to scribble as much as they can remember from their cramming session the night before.

The results, to tell you the truth, are never that great compared to the other work you do during the year. The bottom line is that there is very little chance that your professor will read every word of every answer of every exam that is written (assuming that handwriting would make that possible anyway). Chances are, the professor will look at the first few lines of an answer to see if you have any idea of what you are talking about. Then his eyes will run over the remainder of your mostly illegible answer, but his mind will be thinking of how you presented yourself throughout the year, whether you appeared to be thoughtful or whether you were simply wasting everyone's time.

Despite the fact that all the exams in this stack look more or less the same, and despite the fact that your professor probably hasn't read the entire text of any exam in the pile, the reality is that some of the essays have to receive grades of A, some B, some C, and so on. But how does the professor decide which grades to assign if it is impossible to tell the difference between papers? Well, first, the grade put on your exam will have a lot to do with how well you have followed the advice of this book in order to make yourself someone whom the professor likes and respects. Second, the grade placed on your exam will be dictated by the desire to avoid trouble, so your professor will place a grade that he believes you will not want to appeal, and a grade that, if appealed, can be defended. (Your professor will also want to formulate grades that he believes his department will be willing to accept as proper for a course of that level.) Finally, as we mentioned before, there are some ways that you can communicate to the professor within the exam-writing experience that you are still working with him on a personal level and that, as a result, you feel that he should be responding to you positively when it comes time for him to plunk a number down at the end of your exam.

PLAYING THE GAME—THE THREE-HOUR EXAM DRILL

So let's return to the original scenario. You walk into the exam room after playing the game of professor-student relations like a pro all year. You and the professor both find yourselves playing roles that are different from anything either of you is used to. The situation obviously calls for different behavior. What do you do? You have three hours to answer this question, and your answer will greatly affect how your professor will perceive your work and the grade that you will receive.

The first awkward situation that you will confront is the question of whether, amid the flux of students running to grab the right desk, you are supposed to pause to greet the professor with the usual "hello." Most students, no matter how well they have established their relationship with the professor, do not say anything as they rush past on their way to a seat. They simply behave as though the professor is not there at all. This is a mistake. Obviously, under the circumstances, there is no time or opportunity for the usual exchange of quips, but to let the moment pass without creating any personal contact is foolish. Don't forget, your professors are also quite nervous at this moment; their role in putting you through all this might even make them feel as though they have betrayed you in some way. A very fast, simple greeting will make the necessary contact and let both of you feel as though you are in this together. At this moment, you are communicating the important message that you still like your professor despite this situation that he has put you in.

This greeting can be as simple as smiling at the professor as you pass by on your way to a desk. While smiling and making eye contact, you might even show the professor that you have your fingers crossed or that you have brought your good-luck Snoopy doll, and you and the professor might find yourselves just a little relieved at this very small visual joke. The smallest thing can establish contact, and you will both be less tense afterwards because you have managed to humanize the experience. Your professors will be so overwhelmed by the sight of so many students rushing past them to fill the rows that they will welcome the gesture. This will be the one time when you will appear to have more to say than your professor does.

The only rule to remember is that "Brevity is the soul of wit." Keep it short; keep it light. Never involve the professor in a prolonged discussion at this moment—especially if you want to tell her that you are having a problem, that you are stressed, that you are sick, that you are not ready, that you couldn't understand some of the course material while you were studying. This is not the time. Your professor has a million things on her mind at this moment, and she simply cannot deal with your individual problems. If your problems are genuine, then you can talk about them after the exam when the smoke has cleared and everyone is thinking straight.

At this moment, the key is to make quick contact and grab a seat. If the exam is, in fact, being written in a gymnasium, try to take a seat that is directly in front of the professor, about halfway down the aisle. (You don't want to be too close, or you will run the risk of involving the professor in your stress throughout the exam—too far back or to the side and you will be overlooked entirely.) You will want to be positioned where the professor can see you often during the exam, so that she will be reminded regularly of the effort that you are making throughout this experience. If the exam is being written in a smaller setting like a classroom, then sit in the general area where your seat was located in the classroom during the regular year so that when her eyes drift from place to place (there is nothing more boring than supervising a three-hour exam), you will be exactly where you have always been, and she will be reminded that, throughout the year, you have been a comforting and helpful presence.

TWENTY QUESTIONS

There is one in every crowd; every time any class sits down to write an exam, there is guaranteed to be one student in the class whose hand is raised constantly. This student will force the professor to run up and down the aisle 50 times (the most exercise many professors get all year). The questions burning in this student's mind are usually something like "When it says that we should write our answer in essay form, does that mean, like, in essay form or only, like, in sort of essay form?" or "Should I use a pen or a pencil while writing this exam and, if a pen, what color should the ink be?"

DON'T BE THAT STUDENT!

Despite the fact that you should limit yourself in terms of how many times you raise your hand during the exam, there is no denying that your right to ask one or maybe two questions can offer you yet another good opportunity to make personal contact with the professor while you are writing the exam. You might even want to plan to put your hand up once to draw the professor's attention your way even if you don't really have a question that you desperately need to ask. If, on the exam, the professor has asked you to write about an issue that you dealt with in class from several different points of view (let's say a theory that has been disputed by multiple thinkers), you can call the professor over to ask something like, "Do you want us to get into the specifics of every approach or were you thinking more of a general overview?" This question makes the professor aware of your level of engagement in the topic, it works to establish contact between you and him and, most importantly, it does not compromise the professor by asking for privileged information that he cannot give to everyone else in the class.

The worst kind of question that you can ask during an exam is something like "I can't remember the name of that guy who wrote about supply-side economics. Who was he?" This makes the professor uncomfortable because you are exposing your own ignorance and because the professor is not allowed to give you the answer. In the end, the professor will resent you and regret either answering the question or not answering the question. It would be much more effective to ask something like, "I can't remember the name of that guy who wrote about supply-side economics. Is it okay if I just refer to him as 'that guy who wrote about supply-side economics'?" At this point the professor will probably just give you the name gladly, because you have not compromised either yourself or him in the exchange. You have used humor to make contact and to get the information that you need.

Once the professor is at your desk and you are already talking to him, it is possible to establish closer contact and remind him of your positive engagement with the course. For example, if the professor has taught an author or a text during the course of the year that is obviously a personal favorite of his, chances are he will ask you to write about that author or text somewhere on the exam. When the professor comes over to answer your question, you can always point to that question and say something like, "I knew you would ask about this" with a wry grin on your face. Or if that text is not on the exam, you can, again smiling, ask where it is. In doing so, you will be telling the professor that you are familiar with his areas of specialization. In order to pull this kind of maneuver off, though, you must be fairly confident that you have, in fact, established personal contact over the year. Otherwise the professor will wonder who you are and why you think you are being funny at that moment.

BETWEEN THE LINES

Another way you can try to establish personal contact with the professor while you are writing your exam is to take the opportunity to write one personal joke or comment within the text of your exam answer. For example, if you are writing your answer on an idea that the professor, during lectures, obviously seemed to feel strongly about, you can make contact by joking that you know you are within the professor's personal territory: "The main spokesperson for supply-side economics in the 1980s (and, of course, the greatest thinker of all time, ha! ha!) was . . ." This type of joke shows that you were listening in class, that you have clicked with the professor, and that you are close enough to the professor and the course to understand her own intellectual quirks.

Once again, if you are going to attempt a little joke in the text of your exam, there are two rules to follow. First, one joke or personal comment is enough; don't try to turn your exam into "Evening at the Improv," or your efforts will be obvious and annoying. Second, you should only try to establish humorous contact in the text of your exam if your humor has been successful with this professor on previous occasions; otherwise, your efforts will appear strained, and the professor will wonder what gives you the right to assume this kind of familiarity.

THE LONG GOODBYE

In every class there are some students (around 10 percent of the class) who will take the time to write one or two lines at the end of their exams to wish the professor goodbye and to comment on the course or on their performance on the exam or whatever. Because these final statements are relatively rare, the professor is usually surprised to see them. In the case of students who have made themselves very familiar to the professor over the course of the year, the professor will sometimes be surprised not to receive a farewell note.

These farewell notes written at the end of an exam are tricky, and there is no telling how the professor will receive them.

HARRY: There have been times in my own career where I have read all the answers on a student's exam and had a grade of around 75 percent or so in mind. Then, after reading a particularly nicely worded farewell message by a student toward whom I was sympathetic, I have struggled with the grade and ultimately raised it to the 80 percent range. (Where subjectivity is in play, we can juggle the percentage of various answers to find our target grade no matter how much each of the questions on the exam is worth in the overall score! Yes, it happens all the time.)

But the opposite can also happen; often these notes are written by students who have not said a word all year or who have made a bad impression in some way, and the message is something clumsy like "Sorry about the messy handwriting. I could have said more but I ran out of time. Good course." In these cases, students are usually coming into the exam well out of the A range, and the lackluster note does nothing to raise them up to a higher level. It only further exposes their distance from the professor and from the course. The professor, who has probably not read everything the student has written on the exam anyway, will only be reminded of the student's mediocrity at this crucial moment, and the grade, no doubt, will fall somewhere very close to the student's average for the entire year. (Whether they are aware of it or not, most professors will use the final exam grade to raise the final grade of a good student, and to maintain the status quo of a poor or average student.)

In order to attempt the farewell note, you must be certain that the professor, at least to some small extent, knows and likes you, and that you have made at least a decent showing in the course and on the exam. The text of the farewell note must be handled carefully as well. Keep it short, keep it light, and make sure it flatters the professor without appearing sycophantic. Never use the farewell note to expose the weaknesses of your performance in the course or on the exam. A good note would read something like, "I just wanted to write a quick note to tell you that I really enjoyed the course, and I hope you have a great summer. See you next year." A bad note might read, "Sorry I missed so many classes. I was sick. I think I managed to answer most of the questions on the exam anyway." The first note touches the professor on a personal level; the second reminds the professor of shortcomings in your performance that you should have dealt with long before the exam.

What you must remember is that this note is the last impression you will make on your professors before they place a number next to your name. If you already have a good relationship with the professor, this is a great chance to remind her quickly and subtly of that fact. You will want, at this instant, to remind her that she likes you as a student and that you have feelings that will be affected by the grade you receive. If you haven't done anything all year to establish contact with the professor, anything that you write in the final note will remind her of that fact, and the best that you can do in this case is say nothing and keep her impressions of you neutral.

THE AFTERMATH

When the exam sitting comes to an end and students are rushing away to their freedom, you probably should avoid talking to the professor as you leave the exam room. Once again, a quick smile is the best you can hope for at this frantic moment. If there is an issue that you need to address with the professor, catch him in his office in the hours following the exam rather than trying to have a real discussion in the midst of the chaos. The postexam office chat is the best time to comb out any problems that you might have had in the course and to make contact one last time before the professor sits down to grade that pile of exams.

If you did have problems in the course or on the exam, then it might not be a bad idea to make one last stab at establishing some kind of contact with the professor. In his office after the exam, the professor will probably be feeling relieved that the pressure of the exam experience and the course is over, and he will be more receptive to anything that you have to say. You can even start this quick meeting with a statement like, "I didn't want to bother you in the exam room, but I had a bit of a problem with the middle section of the exam. You see, I missed some of the classes on that subject because . . ." At this point, the professor will be able to listen to what you have to say without feeling pressured, and he'll take any small amount of sympathy you manage to establish during this meeting directly into the grading of your exam.

FINALLY

You walk into the foreign setting of the gymnasium in which you will be writing your exam. Suddenly, the familiarity you have established with your professor is gone, and you find it very difficult even to say a quick hello to her. At this moment, you are actually being tested on two separate levels at once: the first is the written examination on the desk before you, and the second is the test of whether or not you can succeed in making some form of contact with the professor this one last crucial time. Though you only have two or three hours in which to work, there are several little tricks you can try to make the professor aware that you are still the same familiar, friendly, positive presence that you have been all year. One or two friendly words spoken quickly before or during the exam will humanize both you and the professor at this dehumanizing moment. A brief joke or personal message written into the exam might remind the professor of your familiarity at the all-important instant when she has to put a grade on the exam. A short visit soon after the exam can plant a positive seed in the professor's mind that could translate into a slightly higher grade. All these tricks have been known to work at times, but must be handled carefully. Despite the immense pressure of the exam experience (and nothing that we can tell you will alleviate this pressure), you must find a way to let the professor know at some point that you are still the same positive presence you have been all year, and that you are still responding positively to her.

** ORAL PRESENTATIONS **

We thought that while we were talking about how to finesse your essays and exams, those submissions that the professor grades in isolation from your charming presence, we should probably make mention of those instances where it is precisely the nature of your presence that is being evaluated.

TALKING A GOOD GAME

Just in case the normal pressures of your university education don't cause enough stress, there will come a time during your undergraduate career when, much to your chagrin, you will find yourself in the spotlight, standing up in front of your professor and a group of your peers, trying to hold their attention while you deliver a presentation on some important issue like the causes of World War I or the question of whether or not *The Adventures of Huckleberry Finn* is a racist novel. And, while you hope that the words coming out of your mouth will sound like a carefully formulated and sensitive study of a serious academic problem, the thoughts that will be going through your head will be more in the realm of, "Oh my God, is that dandruff on my sleeve? Can anyone see that?" or "Why did the professor just write something in her notebook? Did I say something wrong? Should I take it back? What are they smiling at? Something feels like it's flickering in my nose—what is that? I wonder how fast I can get to the exit?"

Although some of your professors will be content to base your entire grade on traditional written assignments such as essays and exams, others will demand, at some point during the school term, that you stand up before the entire class and present your ideas on a particular topic orally. This exercise, in certain respects, is twice as hard as any written assignment; your grade, in theory, is determined not only by the quality of your ideas and research skills, but by your ability to deliver those ideas eloquently and entertainingly as well. The oral presentation is much different than the class participation grade; in the oral presentation, you don't simply respond to the professor—instead, you become the professor.

Professors have different reasons for putting their students through this grueling ordeal. Professors will tell you that it is a good experience, preparing you for the kind of tasks that you will have to tackle in graduate school or "the real world" (like a professor might know anything about the real world). But for many professors, the oral presentation is also a great way to force a student to do the work that they themselves have been hired to do; it effectively eats into lecture time, so the professor just doesn't have to work as hard. All right, to be fair (grudgingly), some professors are interested in what their students actually have to say, and the presentation can be effective in forcing a student to grapple with an issue. But it does make for an easier ride for the professor, sitting quietly in the seat of judgment and watching the minutes tick off toward the end of class.

For some students, the oral presentation can be one of the most fearful and harrowing experiences of their university careers. We have even known students who have passed up opportunities to take great classes simply because they knew there was a seminar involved, and they were afraid to put themselves through the ordeal. Many students are overwhelmed by the classroom setting, and are content to hide quietly in the corner class after class. These are the students who will have the most trouble stepping forward and commanding their fellow students' attention during a presentation. These are also the students who will not reap the benefits of mastering the subjective aspect of grading. They will remain wallpaper.

Difficult as it may seem, the oral presentation is a great opportunity for the student to step forward and distinguish herself. It can be a very powerful moment because of the attention it commands. If you milquetoast it instead of milking it, the mediocre impression you create will be hard to shake, and mediocrity will be what you'll get back in your grades (not only for the presentation itself, but for the rest of your work in the course). It could be the most important 15 or 20 minutes in the course.

After a great oral performance, it will be very difficult for your professor to see you as anything but an A-level student, even if the rest of your work is less spectacular.

HARRY: I remember a particular class, in which two students presented their oral seminars in subsequent hours. The first student was obviously quite nervous, and offered a long, drawn-out, unorganized discussion (complete with little cue cards flying in every direction). Almost every important word was mispronounced, including the names of the authors being analyzed! This impression on me was lasting, and the work that she handed in subsequent to this presentation—work that may have, for a student who gave a stronger presentation, received a B—was graded below the class average because of that prior experience and the negativity associated with her name.

The next student stood up and offered a presentation that was fast-paced, commanding, and dynamic. Not only did this student receive an A+ for this impressive-sounding speech, but she all but guaranteed herself one of the highest final grades in the class (which she eventually did receive). The reason for this was that she gave me the impression that she knew her stuff quite well. In fact, her ideas may not have necessarily been that much better than those of the first student; what mattered in this case was that she had figured out what professors want from these assignments, and she found a way to play it right.

THE INSIDE TRACK

Before attempting any oral presentation, it is of absolute importance that you make an appointment to meet with the professor in her office at least one week prior to your presentation to talk over your subject and the general design of your discussion. That way, if your argument is way off base (which usually means it contradicts the argument that the professor plans to give on your topic in a subsequent class), then you can try to bring your ideas more in line with hers or at least be prepared for her opposition and fashion your argument more carefully. This is again a time when you need to figure out your professor a little bit: some professors like their ideas to be challenged and discussion to be promoted in the conflict. Others may perceive a seminar that challenges their perspectives as a threat to their authority in the eyes of the rest of the class, and will be insecure enough to come after you for it. The office meeting will let you know with which (head)case you're dealing.

More importantly, by talking to the professor prior to your presentation, you will get a sense of whether there is anything wrong with the overall plan of your discussion. Don't forget, your professor earns a living by lecturing to groups of people, so she will be able to recognize if there are flaws in the organization of your presentation—or if your discussion is in danger of floating off into oblivion with no hope of returning to its focus (which is disastrous if you are actually trying to hold the other students' attention).

Chances are, once your professor has a sense of what you want to say in the presentation, she will begin to offer some suggestions, and in the course of offering these suggestions she may even tell you more than half of what she wants or expects to hear during your presentation. So sit back, listen carefully, and keep a pen and paper ready to scribble any clues that are unwittingly dropped in your lap. Simply by speaking off the top of her head, she will give you a sense of the order your presentation might follow, and she will likely hit most of the major categories she feels you should cover in your discussion. Most professors respond favorably to ideas that resemble their own without actually being their own ideas. Their agreement with your perspective, which has been shaped by their perspective, will make for a harmony that will carry over into the determination of your grade. It will also be harder for a professor to judge you harshly if you are only following the advice that she provided.

THERE'S NO BUSINESS LIKE SHOW BUSINESS

A big part of any successful presentation (and the main thing that distinguishes it from any other assignment) is showmanship. If you put everyone in the room to sleep while delivering your ideas, the quality of your analysis won't really matter. While this book is not designed to teach you how to do better work or how to be a more effective speaker, there are certain tricks that you can use under these circumstances that will certainly impress any professor, whether or not your ideas are as extraordinary as you would like the professor to believe.

There is nothing more painful than watching a student who doesn't seem to know any of the little tricks of handling the pressure of the oral presentation. We all know the different types of students who just can't seem to get it right in front of the group. There is, of course, the Droner, who reads the entire seminar, word for word, from a typed sheet, sounding much like a guilty politician reading a prepared statement to the press. And the Thoroughbred, who talks so fast that you almost feel like you're watching a prize pony racing toward the finish line in the Kentucky Derby. And who could forget the Digger, who spends the entire period of the presentation rooting through a stack of papers for that one ever-elusive page or quotation that will finally make it all make sense? Then there is the Audiovisual Slave, who, while giving a discussion on, for example, the history of the Civil War, will make the class listen to the extended version of the song "War, What Is It Good For?" because "that song really puts it all in perspective." And finally, there's the Blob: the speaker so nervous and jittery that all visible regions of skin are slowly taken over by deepening red blotches (a process much like a car accident, in that those in the vicinity can't help watching in distracted awe).

LIGHTS, CAMERA, ACTION

So the big question remains, what tricks can you use in your presentation if you simply do not feel comfortable in front of the class? What can you do to impress the professor beyond actually improving your oral or academic skills? First, begin your seminar by saying something like "I really have lots of material to get through here, so I'm going to have to move through some of these points a little quickly—please stop me if you need me to slow down and explain any of this." Once you have opened with a statement like that, you have given the professor the sense not only that you are in charge of the group and in command of the material, but also that you have done so much research that there is not even enough time to get through it all.

However, you will, in this event, have to be prepared for a possible interruption and question—but this is not a bad thing. Someone else's question will change the pace for a moment, give everyone a chance to reorient themselves (they've likely started drifting), and give you a chance to demonstrate that you are flexible. This will create the impression that you have truly absorbed the material and can range within it in a way that is more advanced than that of students who appear to need to follow a linear process to the end. And, if someone does interrupt, you really don't need to worry about being thrown. Even if you can't really answer the question, a look of consideration and a response that suggests that the question is interesting and might need to be addressed are good enough to create the impression you need. By making this kind of an opening statement, you will have given the professor the sense that you are actually communicating your ideas rather than just laboring through the ordeal.

A second way that you can improve the reaction to your seminar is to subtly give the impression that you are talking mainly to your professor during your discussion—make eye contact throughout the room, but make certain that your ideas comment on important points that the professor has made in previous lectures. If, for example, you are discussing the involvement of the

North in the American Civil War, and if the professor had previously given his opinion on the political motivations of the North's involvement in the war, then you could easily make a point that quickly and effortlessly integrates the professor's own opinion into your presentation: "When the North got involved in the Civil War—which, as we already know, was more a result of political motivations than a real commitment to the abolitionist cause—its initial military strategy was to attack . . ." and so forth. At the moment that you are integrating the professor's opinion into your discussion, you can even try to flash a quick, knowing glance toward the professor to reinforce the sense that your discussion represents an exchange of ideas and has come out of your consideration of his opinions.

Also, make use of questions. As I said, a question will break up the monotony of a single-person presentation and allow people to regroup and get back into what you were saying. Don't be offended by drifting; peoples' attention spans just aren't that long, and they need variety (of tone and pace) to keep them into it. So pause at key moments or at natural transitional times in your discussion, and ask a question about the other students' opinions on the material that you are presenting. This can be as simple as asking whether or not anyone in the class has anything to add to the points that you have already made. By doing this, not only will you appear to have involved the entire group in your discussion, but the atmosphere of the room will become less formal and stifling. You are not, after all, an authority figure, but a student talking authoritatively to students, and it will make you look even better if you can involve the other students in the process.

Of course, if you are going to attempt the midseminar question, you must always have an answer to your own question ready in case no one responds—if you don't prepare an answer you'll be left with a very uncomfortable or potentially damaging silence. Again, these techniques are understood by the professor as indications of comfort with the material, and the positive overall impression created through them attaches itself to you and your work in general.

THE LOB

Ever been to see a sideshow hypnotist? Ever wonder if those people dancing like chickens or singing "Thriller" with their hands on their groins are for real? Well, real or not, there's a trick in there to be learned. A particularly effective technique to impress your audience, and especially your professor, is to use something that we call "the potted plant." Before the class begins, get a familiar and friendly classmate to ask the perfect question—a question that you have supplied and that she can ask at a key, predetermined moment in your presentation. You will of course be able to knock this lob out of the park, while all stare on in wonder. But don't feel you have to be underhanded about "the potted plant"—you and your friend can make it humorously obvious that the question was planted, thus adding irony and even some theatricality to your presentation. When the question comes up, make a joke of it: "Why, I'm glad you asked that very appropriate question at this key moment in my seminar!" The rest of the class, including the professor, will see the obvious humor of the situation, but you will still have the chance to answer the question and show how much you know about the topic. It will also become obvious that you have involved other people in the class in your work and the formulation of your ideas, which is, really, the point of the exercise.

RISING ABOVE THE GROUP

Some professors may give you the option to present your seminar as a group project rather than on your own. Just keep walking. You're bound, in such situations, to get stuck with a weak link in the class who will try to take advantage of the system by getting everyone else to do his work for him. This will put you in a very uncomfortable position, since you will look like a squealer if you speak to the professor privately, and you will feel like a sucker if you actually end up completing the leech's work for him. Although the group deal is tempting because it diffuses the spotlight, that diffusion is also its major weakness. Remember that the entire point of the class presentation for you is to step forward as an individual; the group situation makes this quite difficult.

The seminar or class presentation is a great chance for you to establish an identity with the professor—a well-presented semi-nar can create a lasting impression on the professor that will di-rectly influence her expectations and her opinions of your future work. And if nerves start to get the better of you, remember what Marcia Brady was told when she took her driver's exam: just pic-ture them in their underwear.

APPENDIX 1

* * *

Stepping on the Lowest Rung

HOW TO PLAY THE TA

It's the first day of classes in your first year of college. You shuffle down the halls, still groggy from the rigors of Orientation Week, and you throw open the doors to the lecture theater. Your eyes gaze over rows of students that stretch out into the distant reaches of the yawning space. At the head of the room, facing you, facial features barely perceptible without binoculars, your professor, whose name you can't quite remember, tries to be heard above the roar. Scattered throughout this classroom, though they might be found sitting smugly in the front row, are people with quite a different stake in this particular course. Though the professor has the master class list, these others will be holding little lists of their own—your name is on one of those lists. Meet your TA.

At some point in your university career (usually in the first year when you are taking introductory courses), you will encounter this strange creature called the teaching assistant (TA). Unlike the professor, the TA will pretty much look like you, dress like you, and talk like you. This TA, also unlike the professor, will probably cheer for the same sports teams as you (or at least cheer for *a* sports team). These people may listen to the same music as you and your friends, and will even know how to use the same slang terms as you—the same slang that the aging professors try to pull off to show you how "hip" they are, only to end up looking like complete dorks (remember our reference to your parents dancing to Pearl Jam?). Although you can identify to some extent with the TAs, you will also sense that there is a distance between you and them, and you will probably find yourself confused in trying to understand what role they play in your life.

What we have said in this book about the importance of your relationships with your professors is equally true of your relationship with your TA. In courses where your professor handles only the lecturing, it is your TA who will come up with the number to be put beside your name. He may be in the lowest position on the professional totem pole, and he may have to answer to higher powers, but if you do not treat him properly, you could end up paying dearly.

PLAYING THE TA

If you thought the professor was an unpredictable beast, wait until you get a look at the TA. Pulled between the poles of student and professor, and really of neither place, the TA is a shape-shifting enigma wrapped in a riddle with no punch line. Playing the TA to your advantage will require the same kind of character analysis that playing the professor requires. You've got to determine what kind of person you're dealing with (on any given day), and what kinds of techniques are going to be the most effective. There are any number of different personality profiles here. Think of yourself as Fox Mulder trying to get into the head of a serial killer (any psychological resemblance to TAs is purely coincidental); you've got to figure out how this person thinks and how to anticipate her needs and desires (and believe us, TAs are a needy and desirous bunch).

But of this be certain: though they may have never stood at the front of the class and though they may have never graded an assignment before, they do have power. They have the power to decide your destiny by assigning grades that will remain with you for the rest of your life! Grades that will affect what programs you will be accepted into in the future! Grades that will influence what jobs you will be hired for! Though their possession of this power seems almost unimaginable, this is the reality of the TA experience, and you must understand who this person is, what makes her tick, and how the classroom looks to her eyes.

A TA IS BORN

Although your professors have probably worked through at least four years of undergraduate studies and at least six years of graduate studies to earn the right to lecture authoritatively to you on their chosen topic and to tell you what grade they think you deserve, the TA's ascent to that same position has been rather abbreviated. Perhaps only a few months before becoming your "teacher," the RA was sitting in an undergraduate classroom much like yours and trying to figure out how she, too, could get the best undergraduate grades out of her professors. With her undergraduate days numbered and graduation quickly approaching, like everyone else, your TA probably started to panic, wondering what her next step in life should be and scrambling to come up with a good emergency plan.

Then, at some point, a professor or a friend or a recruitment poster might have encouraged her to send in an application to a graduate program somewhere. The future TA thinks, "Why not? I've got no plans for the next few years." As one comedian puts it, graduate school is "the snooze button of life," and it's pressed by the person begging for "just two more years! Please, just two more years!" before having to "wake up" and go out into the cold, hard world.

Eventually, a letter of acceptance arrives from a graduate school, and with the acceptance comes an offer of a TA position. All of a sudden a compromise with real life can be achieved; the future TA thinks, "I can go to school and have a job too." And, though the money is just barely enough to survive, it is usually more than this person has ever been offered for anything even remotely connected with her area of study. Now she can finally tell her parents and people at parties that she's working in her chosen field.

The fact that this person has been accepted to do graduate studies does not necessarily mean that she was an outstanding undergraduate; as we've told you, learning how to push the right buttons and play the game well is a large component—your TA might simply be someone who learned this more quickly than most. In fact, the only advantage that your TA might have over you is that she may have taken your course before as an undergraduate. Or, it might be just as likely that (like many professors) she has never even taken an undergraduate course in the subject area that she is teaching, and she has to learn the material at the same time as her students. This, as you can imagine, is a very intense experience.

The new TA, like you, arrives at the university in September. He meets for an hour or two with the professor he'll be working under, he receives a few words of instruction or encouragement, and then he's abruptly plunked down in front a group of students who look an awful lot like he did way back in . . . June! Some of these new ones find the whole thing kind of cool, but most, at least during the first few classes, feel like they are sinking fast.

HARRY: In my own first class as a TA (I can't believe I'm telling you this), I decided to break the ice by having each of my students announce to the rest of the group who his or her favorite Beatle is. It was 1989! My students stared at me like I was from another planet. Another TA (you see, it's not just me) spent the first three classes of the year biding time by asking all his students where they came from and whether they missed their home town.

The truth is that if you can figure out a way to help your TA through this agonizing time, if you can come up with the right comment to get her through this harrowing moment, or the phrase that will let her know that you have accepted her in her role as teacher, not only will she probably come to see you as a comforting presence in her life—she may in fact accept you as her savior.

YOU THINK YOU'RE THE ONLY ONE WITH PROBLEMS?

The problem of establishing himself as an authority figure in the classroom setting is only one of the difficulties in the life of a TA as he begins to work for the hardest $8,000 (generous average) he will ever earn. In fact, there are many other pressures and issues in his life that will affect the ways in which you might interact with him.

The most important thing that you need to remember is that TAs are, first and foremost, students. Their priority will almost always be their own work, and they have tons of it. While some will take the tutorials they instruct or the papers they grade very seriously, most are just worried about time: in the case of the TAs who merely grade papers, they're worried that the papers are going to take too long to grade (which they do) and keep them from their own ever-present work, and, in the case of the teaching TAs, in addition to the worries about grading time, they're also worried they won't have 50 minutes worth of stuff to say (and they'll blame you if they fall short). Basically the TA just wants to get back to one of four places: the library (keener intellectual), the research laboratory (nasal whiner), home (recluse), or the graduate pub (career student). So, for TAs, like the professor, getting in the way is the worst thing you can do. Yes, they're being paid to provide you with a certain service, but the less you ask of them (and the more they realize how little you ask of them), the more inclined they will be in your favor.

At the same time, because TAs are students, they can be encouraged to sympathize with you if you make it evident that you sympathize with them. One of the most common complaints of graduate students is that very few people understand what they're doing. Their families, unless there's a professor among the relatives already, don't really understand what graduate school is about; people at parties smile politely but don't really know what it means to be in graduate school; and, if the students are in their first year of graduate studies, their romantic partners are soon to be their romantic partners no longer (graduate school has all the aphrodisiac potency of pepper spray).

So the student who can fill this void and offer respect to the disrespected, appreciation to the unappreciated, and understanding to the misunderstood will find herself in a special position of protected association (that elusive inner circle that we told you about).

DRESSED IN A LITTLE BRIEF AUTHORITY

On the issue of respect, the TA has power. Never underestimate this. If you have a problem with authority, or a problem with someone so seemingly inexperienced having authority over you, well, you better get over it because this is your life for the duration of the course. You can take a little comfort in the fact that the TA is not operating completely unsupervised, but remember what we told you about professors and their desire to lead undisturbed lives—the attention paid by a professor to a TA is usually minimal, and the checks and balances in place to check and balance TAs are fairly superficial. Typically, there is a weekly meeting at which that week's tutorial subject or demonstration is briefly discussed, but there is rarely attention paid to things like how the TA is conducting his office hours and advisory role or how he is grading. So the TA is given a large amount of room—or, if you prefer, enough rope to hang himself. His sense of authority, particularly as a new kid in town, is fairly fragile, and a student who challenges it might feel the sting of the backlash as the TA struggles to re-establish classroom dominance.

CHAIN OF COMMAND

DAVID: One year, once upon a time when I was a TA, I had a student in one of my tutorials who I just couldn't reach. He thought I was a dim-witted geek with nothing to tell him that he didn't already know, and he made no secret of his contempt for me as I stood in front of my other students. Well, what he didn't know was that, dim-witted or not, he was stuck with me, and that burning his bridges with me meant falling into the icy cold waters below. Without trying first to work it out with me, he decided to go over my head and complain to the professor leading the course—the same professor who had known and liked me for at least three years and who had no idea who this guy was.

While this stranger complained about me, the professor listened, all the time looking at his watch and thinking, ''How do I get this guy out of my office and back on my TA's plate?'' He nodded to the student, acknowledged his concerns and then told him that he's known me for three years and always found

me to be reliable and . . . yadda yadda yadda. The professor
promised to ''look into'' the student's concerns, and he sent
the student on his way.

When, at the next meeting, I found out that this professor
had been bothered (and as a result was now thinking of me as
less than perfect and as the source of some small disturbance
to his sanctum) because of one of my students, I was not thinking of the teaching or grading issues involved—I was thinking
that I'd been made to look bad in front of a person whose opinion of me was crucial to my career, and I was thinking that a
certain student in my tutorial had leapt from the frying pan
into the fires of hell.

The proverbial woman scorned doesn't have anything on a
wounded TA. If you embarrass or compromise your TA in front
of his supervisor-professor, his own grades and future might be
threatened, and his sense of the ensuing loss of respect in his
department will come back to you, quite literally, with a
vengeance.

Now this is not to say that you can't have differences of opinion with your TA or that you have to take his word as final in all
cases. What it does mean is that his power over you is real, that
he deserves respect, and that he must be treated professionally at
all times, even if you think he's a professional moron. Graduate
schools are intensely competitive: graduate students are always
being compared and ranked, and infighting is frequent, as are
attempts to embarrass or sabotage each other. The fragile and ten-
uous position of the TA in his department is actually an advantage
to students—his lack of confidence and need for reassurance mean
that he'll welcome and encourage, and reward, those that make
him feel better about his knowledge and abilities. TAs feel lowly
because they're often treated as lowly by professors and administration, but if you can make them feel a little stronger by respect-
ing their place in the order of things, your place in the order of
things is likely to rise.

VISITATION RITES

TAs, like professors, usually have to schedule office hours. Use
these hours. Of course, use them with the kind of discretion we

suggested in Chapter 4: visiting not too often and not on the brink of the end of the period, reading the signs of welcome or anxiety and acting accordingly, becoming personal only when encouraged to do so, and suggesting through word and deed that this person is interesting and her subject engaging. You might even ask her about being a TA because you think you'd like to go to graduate school—though, if you do this, prepare yourself for a litany of complaints. (Just keep telling yourself that your TA's willingness to complain to you is a sign of comfort and familiarity—exactly where you want to be when it comes to the grading of your work.)

Keep in mind, though, that the office hours for TAs are, most of the time, hours they simply blow off. They know nobody is usually going to show up, and so they use the time for scheduled malingering. The best thing about graduate school is the hanging out. The TA gets an office on campus, and he thinks that's pretty cool. Usually the office is shared with other TAs, and is located in a hall with the offices of still more TAs, so it's like a neighborhood: it becomes the place of witty banter, drop-in inquiries both personal and professional, sexual escapades, political wrangling, and grumbling about work and co-workers. The TA, although complaining about the waste of time that goes on in these halls and offices, loves it (at least until about her fourth year). So don't be seen as the spoiler. When you come by, show appreciation for her little niche—and if it looks like she is aware that something fun is brewing somewhere else, let her go relatively quickly. Obviously, you'll want to address the questions that brought you there, but try to do so efficiently (even if this means a follow-up visit next time) so that she sees you as understanding and sympathetic—one of the good ones.

CROSSING PATHS

Because TAs are still students (and usually younger than your professors), you are more likely to have accidental contact. You're more likely to bump into them in the halls, in the library, even in the bar downtown, than you are your regular professors (those who have ceased to have a life). Make the most of these opportunities, but that also means not making too much of them. Your TAs want you to recognize and like them, so, when you run into them outside of the class, go up and say "hello" and tell them who you are. Don't pull your chair up to their table in a restaurant or anything, but give them the chance to acknowledge you. They may chat a bit, or they may brush you off—be open to both responses.

To professors or TAs, the awareness of one or more of their students in a bar or restaurant can be a bit inhibiting. We and a group of close colleagues used to meet every Thursday night (at the very least) in this downtown bar. It was a small but popular spot and was usually in full bustle by midnight. Invariably, among the patrons would be a student whom one of us had in tutorial or lecture. Whoever had the student would lean across the table, gesture in the student's direction, and tell the others, "There's one of my students."

This would be the point where, if the student was known or had done something particularly distinguishing, the gossip would start to fly. If the student was rather unmemorable, the topic would immediately die. In either case, though, expectant in the minds of all those at our little academic table was that the student would wander over for a "hello." If she didn't, we'd consider that a snubbing, and whoever was responsible for the student would begin wondering what was behind this insult. At the same time, none of us wanted the student to become part of our evening's festivities; we were there for escape, and the student's presence in the room meant that we were already partly compromised—if one of us fell off a chair, spilled a beer, or sang the "Piers Plowman" song too loud, we knew the whole tutorial would know by the next meeting.

So there are a couple of things in play here. The student's acknowledgment is a point of pride at the table—the student comes over, says "hello," chats warmly for a few moments, and moves on, leaving the other TAs at this table thinking their friend has developed good relationships with his students. This enhanced sense of worth at the table has a reciprocal effect in his remembrance that it was you who made him look good in front of his friends. But the reverse is also true: a snub or too much familiarity from a student can bring tension into this bar scene, the place where these TAs have all gone to relieve a little tension. And the student responsible for this changed environment might find TAs deciding to introduce a little tension into the one environment that is in their control—the classroom.

I'M NEW HERE

Remember, the reason that you are more likely to run into your TAs in the outside world is that they are often within four or five years of your age and therefore still share some interests in common with you. So, imagine you were asked to grade a classroom's essays—how would you do it? Truth is, the young TA usually has absolutely no idea how to mark an essay or an exam. Never having participated in this process before, he simply cannot tell the difference between an assignment that deserves an A and one that deserves a C, other than by making mental comparisons to what the paper might have looked like had he, probably an A student prior to graduate school, written it. And yet, there is nothing that this young TA fears more than being exposed to the professor as someone who cannot grade properly.

> **HARRY:** The first time that I was a TA, I was so intimidated by this process that, after the professor in charge told me that my grades should average out at around a 70 percent, I gave all the assignments that I graded somewhere between 68 and 72 percent. When, several months into the school term, one of my students hinted to me that my class was preparing a mutiny (meaning they were going to tell the professor on me), I found the courage to stretch my range a little higher, into the A zone, and a little lower to maintain that all-important 70 percent average.

Once you have discovered that your TA cannot afford to look bad in the eyes of the higher ranking professors under any circumstances, you may find yourself holding the most important wild card in your effort to win that elusive A. Play it carefully.

POLITICAL CORRECTIONS

Graduate seminars, the courses TAs have to take as students, are intense. This intensity makes the environment intimidating. To each graduate student, all the others in the class seem to belong there and seem to be intellectually engaged. Almost all graduate students, if they're encouraged with enough alcohol, will confess to the feeling that they're going to be found out as a fraud. Very quickly, these people realize that they must present themselves as much more critically involved and politically radical than they ever thought they would be (playing their own game). Young graduate students often become outspoken representatives of the first idea that grabs their interest in their first graduate course. Young women and men, who up to this point have lived simple apolitical lives of detachment, emerge as ardent feminists, wry Marxists, ironic poststructuralists, or any combination of a number of "——ists." These identities become very important, and, because they are newly created, they are usually fragile: the student of such neophytes has to be very careful not to throw potentially insulting bombs into these delicately constructed houses of cards.

At the same time, discerning students can use the political interests of their TA to their advantage. The newly committed TAs will likely use their new discoveries wherever possible in your classroom contact with them; watch for this, and act accordingly.

> **DAVID:** I was an easy target as a graduate student: I was the sensitive-guy feminist who didn't know a whole lot about the theories behind contemporary feminism. Students, especially women, picking up on this and writing about issues of gender tended to do better in my tutorials.

Remember though, a little knowledge is a dangerous thing: you must be pretty confident that you know enough about the subject to handle it adequately because this will be a protected area for the TA, and trespassers will be prosecuted. Now, if your particular TA's pet school of thought involves hermeneutical phenomenology, we suggest you just change schools.

A TALE OF TWO TUTORIALS

Younger TAs are usually more approachable, more inclined to open themselves to friendly relationships with their students. They need something in their life that is nonthreatening (who doesn't?), and if you convince them that that's your approach to their role in your life, then they'll let their defenses down and let you into their inner circle.

> **DAVID:** In the second year of my Ph.D., my two tutorial groups were in consecutive time slots: at the end of the first, because of the post-class swarm factor, I had to sprint down the hall, in a whirl of papers and chalk dust, to teach the second. Though culled randomly from the same general class list, the two groups couldn't have been more different. And my attitude to each corresponded to this difference.
>
> The first group was nondescript: no one really stood out, and, except for the occasional spark, they were quiet and bored looking. I would head down the hall to the second group on a low, thinking the tutorial I had just given, the same one I was just about to give to the next group, had been a flop, and I was nervous and feeling rushed. But when I came through the door, all those feelings evaporated. I was greeted with smiles, maybe a joke about cancelling the class, and, once, even a cupcake and a birthday card signed by the whole group. (Okay, so maybe I dropped a hint or two about having to teach on my birthday.) And I knew that the reason this class was such a pleasure was that two of the students made it their job to make it that way. They were always willing to meet me halfway in my tutorials, to offer an attempt when I was struggling to get at something, to not leave me hanging in the breeze.
>
> Occasionally, after a class had been particularly energetic and interesting, they'd tell me that they had had fun, and I always liked hearing it. Eventually, they got me to the place where, when one of them didn't show up (a rare occasion), I was disappointed. In other words, they had me. I looked forward to their presence because they seemed to enjoy mine. And when it came time for me to grade their assignments, it was impossible for me to separate the person from the work, so I always found much to reward.

BEEN THERE, DONE THAT

This willingness to be forgiving of and giving to the TA, while particularly effective with the more junior ones because of their insecurities, will also work with the seasoned TA. And you are bound during the course of your career to run into this category of graduate student, the one who has been loitering and stalling in his program like a mallrat at The Gap. Find out where he is in his graduate studies: while the young TA will normally be doing a master's degree or will be in the first or second year of a Ph.D. program, the older TA will be further along in his Ph.D. program or lingering in the department after finishing. Grad students always like to complain about their work, so ask him to tell you what he's working on.

The older TAs will be easy enough to recognize; they are (and oh so aware of it!) a few years older than you (typically pushing 30, a borderline number they're not anxious to cross). They are also, typically, more confident in front of the classroom. Their clothes were in style when they were undergraduates, which means that by the time you meet them their wardrobe is about three to six years out of style. Whatever financial, social, or professional pressures that the new, young TA has been dealing with for a month or two, these seasoned TAs have been enduring for years. Older TAs, who probably initially entered graduate school to avoid the real world for a short time, have watched the years roll by, during which they have watched all their old friends get real jobs, buy real homes and minivans, and start real lives. Like Rip van Winkle, these TAs have gone into a kind of sleep in the prime of their lives, yet they're condemned to keep waking up to be reminded that the world is passing them by.

The new, younger TAs still believe that there are exciting ideas and endless nuggets of wisdom for them to discover as a graduate student and instructor. In contrast, most older, seasoned TAs are far less enthusiastic and realize that their job is just like any other job, except that it pays about 90 percent less. The more seasoned TAs are starting to become disillusioned with their chosen profession. They encounter the politics and the injustices of the system, and they start to see you as part of that system. Aware that they are being exploited as cheap labor by the professor and by the university, they begin to see you as part of just another pile of essays that they will have to grade. Under pressure about (the absence of) their dissertation (a very dirty word), they imagine they are getting closer and closer to obsolescence. Some will still manage to muster some enthusiasm for their tutorials, but others will be bitter, perhaps resentful, and almost all will be more difficult to reach on a personal level. (It's actually around this time that they start thinking about writing a book like this one.)

YOU MAKE ME FEEL SO YOUNG

For those of you who didn't recognize the above heading as a line from Frank Sinatra, our point should be pretty clear. Aging TAs are starting to lose the common ground with their perpetually young students, and it's bugging them. So instead of sitting back and watching amusedly as they teeter on the brink of falling into the generation gap, you need to reach across to them.

> **HARRY:** The real player of a student would have answered my goofy question about favorite Beatles with the name Yoko Ono. The humor of such an answer would bridge the years between older TA and younger student, and establish an immediate ironic rapport.

Like the young professor, the older TA experiences the double bind of wanting to be part of the system at the same time as she wants to be seen as above or subversive toward it. She is getting the sense that she is moving closer toward the dusty figures she used to make fun of, and so she begins to feel desperate for some recognition of her cool from her younger and captive audience. Exploit this. Many students will roll their eyes at this wannabe, and those eye rolls feel like knives under the robs (not that we speak from any experience here). If you can give her the occasional signal that you see her as still in some way connected or relevant, then she in turn will see you as a perceptive devil with exquisite taste. But when buttering up the seasoned TA, never get caught with greasy hands. Remember, she's seen a few of these classes before, and she'll be wise to the fawning butt kisser. Making references to her "smoldering eyes" might be taking it too far. But letting her know that she is the only "prof" you've got who makes the material interesting to you will be a good way of placing her inside the system while distinguishing her from it.

BUILDING CHARACTER

You will get a sense of the character of your TA quickly. (Well, perhaps we're being too quick to generalize; some TAs have no character whatsoever.) Puzzle him out. Does he think of himself as funny, radical, serious, a hipster? Is his identity wrapped up in being a rights activist (for gays, men, women, ethnic groups, the disabled, animals)? Does he show flexibility in the classroom or is he rigid about time and direction? Like we said in Chapter 4, reinforcing their ideal sense of self is a sure ticket to a person's inner circle of cherished people. If teaching seems to be important to your TA, if he is disappointed when a class doesn't go well or when discussion isn't generated by his questions, then you play on this: make him aware that he's successful, that his love of the material is clear and infectious, or give him an out (tell him that the group wasn't giving much today—must be midterm blahs). You want him thinking that he's engaging you, that you come to his class because you enjoy his presence, and that you think he has something important to contribute. If he believes you have this kind of respect for him, then he will protect that relationship with the kind of grades that ensure his future with you (and your future success).

APPENDIX 2

* * *

Correspondence Courses

LONG-DISTANCE RELATIONSHIPS NEVER WORK

At one time or another, most of us have been there: a job or school takes us to a different city, or perhaps a boyfriend or girlfriend moves away—whatever the situation, the difficulty of the long-distance relationship is well established. There is one practical reason for this difficulty (besides the lack of sex): it is hard to communicate when the other person isn't in the room with you (let's be honest, it's hard enough to make it work when you *are* in the same room). Well, a correspondence course is a kind of long-distance relationship, and it shares some of the same problems.

The correspondence course, like the long-distance relationship, is lousy for both people involved. But it is a particularly hard deal for the student. Removed from the regularly scheduled classroom regimen, studying depends on self-discipline and will-power. Course materials are usually out of date, and if you thought professors could be dull in person, you should hear them on tape. There is also an element of isolation that should not be underestimated. In a classroom of 50 students, you meet people, talk about the course and other things, and exchange impressions of the strange animal at the front of the room, and, when you get your assignments back, it is a shared experience with 49 fellow anxiety sufferers. But the correspondence student gets none of this, and walks to the mailbox having no one to share the dread or confirm the opinion that "this guy's a jerk." Nonetheless, for students in remote locations, or students needing certain credits offered only sporadically, the correspondence course might be the only option. In terms of the importance of the professor-student relationship, what is true of the regular course is also true of the correspondence course: making yourself a familiar and appreciated presence for the professor will take control of the subjective aspect of grading and make it work in your favor.

THE ONLY GAME IN TOWN

We've spent some time in this book telling you that the nature of the relationship you establish with your professor is a significant one in terms of what it can do for your grades. In a correspondence course, your opportunities for contact and relationship building are severely limited. You don't have the classroom, you don't have the office hours, and if you bumped into your professor on the street or in Wal-Mart, you wouldn't even recognize that this was your chance to score some brownie points. (Photographs of professors are rarely included in the course material for correspondence courses, and you have only to attend the next faculty assembly to know why.) You have only a few resources: the telephone, the personal note, and, perhaps, one face-to-face meeting (if you live close enough and are skillful enough). And, as any straight-poker player will tell you, when you get only one hand, you've got to play it very well.

Come to think of it, for the student, the correspondence course is like being a pen pal with a prison inmate. Now, I know that there are people on "Oprah" and "Sally Jessy" who will tell you it works beautifully, but let's face it, in most of those cases, the absence of personal physical contact is working to their advantage. Not so for the student in a correspondence course. Here, the inmate is a highly judgmental professor who receives and grades assignments as if they have arrived out of thin air. You, being the source of that paper, are rarely a real person to this professor. In the absence of the classroom or office contact, the professor has no sense of you as an individual distinct from the other faceless names. And, if you're just a cold number to the professor, then a cold number is what you'll get back, a number unaffected by the inspiration of human warmth.

PLEASED TO MEET YOU; HOPE YOU GUESS MY NAME

The first thing you need to do to overcome these disadvantages is to introduce yourself to the professor. This introduction needs to be handled carefully because, after all, this will be a first and lasting impression. Most of the time, all you will get of the professor in a correspondence course is her name, rank, and serial number. Your assignments are usually sent to a central processing place on campus, and shipped from there to the professor. Also, the professor grading the papers quite often has no responsibility for the course materials—the taped lectures, packaged notes, handbooks, and so on are likely the same ones that have been used for a number of years with a number of different instructors. But once you have the name of the person leading your section of the course, you have a certain amount of control.

It may be the case that you are a regular student at the institution and you are taking the course over the summer while you're back home. In this instance, try to make contact with the professor before you leave the campus for the summer. But make the appearance brief and general—chances are that this professor hasn't even given one thought to the course yet and is still trying to recover from the end of the previous term. Find her during her office hours; tell her that you've heard these courses can be quite isolating and that you just wanted to introduce yourself before returning home. The professor will likely respond in kind, ask where "home" is and what you'll be doing there, and, all of a sudden, you've become a person to her. If she just stares at you as if a large cockroach has just crawled out of your mouth, then say you're looking forward to the course and beat a hasty retreat.

Either way, you've set yourself up as someone who is already thinking about the course, and interested enough to take the initiative to seek out its leader. The value of such personal contact comes into play when your paper arrives one morning in her mailbox and the name on it means something, if only a vague something, when she reads it.

TELEPHONE LINES

If you don't live in the same city as the professor, or you don't want to risk the awkwardness of a cold introduction, then you are left with the telephone—the most intrusive piece of furniture in the professor's home or office. As we told you in Chapter 4, these calls are almost never welcome, so the introduction call is particularly thorny. The best thing to do is wait until the course has officially begun, call up with a specific question that suggests an engaged response to the material, and say "thank you" and "goodbye" before the clock has gone three minutes.

DAVID: A keener student of mine, registered in a course that began in mid-May, called me at home in late April. I had just walked in the door from post-softball tavern-style male bonding, and here's this person dying to tell me all about the productions of Shakespeare he'd seen in England last summer and how he was so looking forward to getting at them in a ''deeper'' way. Now, I'm not an absolute cad; at first I was charmed and I appreciated his genuine enthusiasm. But, as the call passed the ten-minute mark, I grew less and less charmed and started wishing I'd let the machine pick up. I hadn't given the course one moment's thought (other than to calculate what the check for it might look like). I was sweaty and beery and perhaps a bit bleary, and here I had to muster my professorial manner when all I really wanted to do was go back and toast that great catch in left field (one more time).

When you dial the professor's phone number, at home or office, you never know into what situation you are intruding. The phone is risky, and calling before the course has officially started is like reminding someone enjoying youth and beauty that he's going to die.

Though risky, the phone might also be the only way you've got to diagnose your professor's particular character. As we've told you elsewhere, getting a handle on the nature of your professor will be crucial to determining the kinds of things that she wants from you. But the phone can give you only limited information (she might, for instance, through the entire length of your phone call, be rolling her eyes and giving you the finger—you'll never know). Listen for tone—is she welcoming? Abrupt? Relaxed? Sedated? Evaluate whether she sounds young or old, funny or humorless; is she quick to draw conclusions about the material or willing to explore different positions on it? All this information can help you when it comes to producing your essays and/or assignments, and when it comes to deciding on the kinds of things that will help you establish a familiar relationship with her.

Correspondence professors usually have to designate particular hours during which they are to be available for phone calls— so you do have some rights here. But rights aren't going to get you those extra grades—careful exercise of them will. So, by all means, use the appointed hours. But moderation is key. The correspondence professor usually holds "phone hours" from home, so even though these hours are scheduled, they nonetheless are an invasion of his private space. Use them sparingly—only two or three times, in appointed hours, during the term of a summer course, and double that if the course stretches over the regular eight-month period. And never call at unappointed times.

When you do call, imagine that you've just put a succulent piece of beef tenderloin on the barbecue (vegetarian students may substitute tofu), and if you talk too long the thing will become charred. That's the nature of the relationship you've got going here with the professor—too long on the phone and you'll burn it. During the phone call, you become a guest in his home, and the choice is yours: you can leave him with his life intact, happy to have you over again, or you can disrupt his world to the point that the very thought of your name is enough to make him break out in hives. You can even play the call like an office visit and ask, right after you tell the professor who you are, if he's got a minute or if he'd rather you called back at another time. You're showing him that you know the phone is an invasion and that you're trying to be considerate. And the point of the phone call, and the contact, is to show off your good points so that you will score the good points.

Call the professor only when you have a carefully focused question to ask. (Remember, your question should be formed in such way to make the best possible impression.) When the professor has addressed the question to your satisfaction, or after about three minutes (whichever comes first), begin the process of thanks and farewell. Of course, if the professor initiates conversation, then go with it—this is the kind of thing that can really overcome the pitfalls of the correspondence-course relationship. But always keep your responses brief (not abrupt), so that he never has to wait too long before returning to the episode of "Baywatch" he was engrossed in before the phone rang.

NOTABLE NOTES

By definition, the *correspondence* of *correspondence course* means a communication by letters, so there is something appropriate about slipping in a note or two to your professor among your assignments. But, like the phone call, you have to be careful not to overdo it. Think of it from the perspective of the professor: if, with your assignment, you send her a note with a bunch of questions or excuses or responses to the material, then not only are you asking her to evaluate the assignment (do her job) but she is put in a position in which she has to respond to your note (seen as nothing but extra work). Remember that your paper isn't the only one she has to grade, and, while the correspondence course might seem lonely to you, the professor has more than enough company stacking up on her desk. If you're going to add paper to the pile, then you've got to do it in a way that won't be seen merely as adding to the work load.

Don't ever slip a note in with the very first assignment. Wait it out and get more information: your phone call and the comments on your first assignment will help you determine whether or not this professor seems open to communication outside the formal bounds of specified assignments. If you think that there is a certain casual and personal quality to the professor, then you might think about slipping her a note with the second assignment. If, on the other hand, the phone call and the comments on your first work seem coolly professional, then don't use the personal-note technique—it won't be received in a way that will work toward a positive technique—it won't be received in a way that will work toward a positive impression of you. Stick with the brief phone call during specified hours.

The content of your note needs to be carefully prepared. Make it handwritten—typed notes look too official, and you want to make the note a form of communication distinct from the assignment. Make it brief—no more than one paragraph of about five sentences. It might be a question, but it should be a precise one and one that is limited in scope: this isn't the place for general ruminations or questions that require the professor to produce an essay of his own in response. And, as we've told you elsewhere in this book, make it a question that will create the impression that you are engaged with the material at a high level, something like "I really enjoyed the section on B. F. Skinner, but I'm having a little more difficulty with Piaget. Does he think that these stages in psychological development just happen without social conditioning?" All you've done here is gestured at applying the theories of one section of the course to the theories of another, and you've asked a question that can be responded to very quickly by someone well versed in the area.

You might also use this note to show the professor that you take her comments seriously. "I tried to incorporate your advice about taking the argument another step. Please let me know if this is an improvement or if I still need to push it farther." This kind of note tells the professor that you respect her advice and that you are trying to do better by taking her guidance. But don't ever use the note to throw her words back at her: trying to blame her advice for what she later points out as your mistakes will only make the relationship antagonistic. Always accept responsibility and ask for help rather than accuse the professor of misleading you (even if it might be true). Your note should suggest to the professor that you expend effort evaluating and responding to the effort she is making—that her comments are important to you. Such a note will make the professor feel better about the course and about the time she takes to write comments, and that feeling will make her inclined to reward your apparent effort.

UP CLOSE AND PERSONAL

The student who lives in the same city as the professor might be able, during the period of a correspondence course, to finagle a meeting with that professor. We know of one colleague, teaching writing, who happily met with his particularly zealous students in a local coffee shop. He said he didn't mind this meeting because these students were working hard to be better writers. While they may not have been great writers, these students had done a number of things right: they'd convinced their professor of their determination to succeed and revealed their personal investment of time and energy in the course. This in turn made the professor invest in them: he saw them as dedicated, and he appreciated this dedication to the point that he was willing to go a step further to help them. When a professor invests in you to this extent, he or she will find it very difficult to be stingy with grades.

The meeting should take place only if it is truly justified. You might simply call and say, "I wanted to discuss how I might go about correcting some of the mistakes I made on the last paper. I don't want to make the same mistakes again. Is there some time we could meet and go over specific errors with the paper in front of us both?" If the professor deigns to meet you, then you have to bring something to the table that is worth that inconvenience. Prepare for this meeting well—have specific and focused questions and be ready to talk about past problems and future solutions. For instance, bring your last assignment but instead of making the professor justify her criticisms, focus with the professor on correcting these problems for the next assignment.

If the professor doesn't respond well to your call for a meeting, then drop it and never bring it up again. A professor who refuses a meeting will likely feel a little guilty about it (everything aside, his conscience and his professionalism are telling him that he should be willing to do it for the good of the student); if you continue to make the professor feel guilt, then he'll associate you with that negative feeling. When an assignment with your name on it next comes across his desk all he's got to go with it is a sour taste (not a good start to any grading experience).

FINAL WORDS

The final exam in a correspondence course is usually written in a central location. If you are in the same city as the professor, that professor will likely be supervising your examination. This is no time to try to make up for lack of contact during the course. The most that you should do at this stage is say "hello" and "It's nice to finally meet you." But do make sure that she sees your face, catches your name, and makes the connection between you and your work. A carefully timed question during the exam, or some of the other techniques we discussed in Chapter 5, might be enough to secure the connection in the professor's mind. If you've played the game as well as can be, these efforts will be enough to maintain the relationship, and it won't look like you're trying too hard.

MAIL BONDING

Correspondence courses are the weak link in college education. They should be avoided if possible, and, if not, played carefully. Somehow you have to overcome the anonymity of the very design of the course, and to do this requires that you invade what professors might consider their personal space. But a short phone call or a well-thought-out note slipped in with one or two of the assignments can humanize you and make you stand out among that vertical string of student numbers that makes up the correspondence professor's class list. You will never be able to master the subjective aspect of grading in the way that you can in the classroom situation, but you can at least get a portion of the potential power of the professor-student relationship working for your benefit.

APPENDIX 3

* * *

Cramming Session

LAST-MINUTE WORDS OF ADVICE

Letters
- The professors with whom you have taken multiple courses and by whom you've been positively regarded and graded should be your first target when aiming for letters of recommendation. They'll be the ones who can talk about breadth of experience, and they'll also be the ones to feel they have a larger stake in your success. They'll be the ones to write the letters that suggest your outstanding qualities. Such letters will go a long way in your future graduate school and job applications. In other words, once you have created a sympathetic relationship with your professor and earned an A in the process, don't settle for just that single A. Make certain that the professor who sees you as a top-level student plays an even more integral part in your future.

- It might be a good idea to send a letter of thanks to each of your sympathetic professors *after their courses are finished* (that way it doesn't look as though you are sucking up). All you have to say in the note is that you got a great deal out of their course, and that you believe the material you learned will contribute positively to your scholarship in the future (again, professors *love* to feel that their work has benefited you in a permanent way—it gives them the feeling that their ideas will circulate beyond their classroom and become socially relevant, which they see as the ultimate purpose of the academic exercise). You may not think that you have anything to gain by expending the effort of writing this little note, but you never know when you will be taking another course with that professor or perhaps asking her for a letter of recommendation, and no professor ever forgets even so small a gesture as a quick note of thanks. (It is hard to forget it when it is so rarely offered.) This effort, which will take you all of five minutes, could benefit you for a lifetime.

- If you do have to ask a professor for a letter of recommendation, make certain that you are actually asking someone who will have something nice to say about you. (It is not against the rules to directly ask the professor to tell you whether he could comfortably write a strong recommendation for you—he will probably be relieved to tell you the truth and not have to write the letter if he feels that you were less than spectacular in his course.)

- When you ask a professor for a letter of recommendation, give her everything she needs—she shouldn't have to do anything but write the letter. That means you have to give her all the information (like submission deadlines), the correct forms, and a stamped, addressed envelope to use when sending the letter. Not only will this assure that the correct process for your letter takes place, but it will also likely make the letter better. Think about it: if someone asks you for a letter (extra work) and then makes you run around getting information or going to the post office, or even looking up the correct addresses of the institutions, what kind of energy is going to go into the writing of the letter itself? Resentment makes for bad letters.

- After the letter of recommendation has been sent, never forget to write a short, appreciative letter of thanks—chances are, sooner or later, you'll need to hit her up for another one. Even though some professors regard these letters as their duty, it is always nice for them to know that their work has been appreciated.

ANOTHER ROUND PLEASE

- If you have followed the advice offered in this book, and you have succeeded in raising your grade by developing a sympathetic relationship with a particular professor (meaning that the professor has already given you a solid A grade and definitely sees you as being capable of great work), then by all means, keep taking courses with that professor in subsequent terms. Once a professor has given you that first A, it becomes harder to lower your grade in subsequent courses because you have already established yourself as a top student, and he will not want to have to admit that he was wrong about you the first time around. By the time that you have taken multiple courses with a professor, you and that professor will have experienced mutual evolution—he's changed as a teacher, and you've changed as a student. This creates a sense that the two of you are developing in some way together, and it can give the professor an inflated sense of his role in your future success. We still correspond with some of the professors who taught us in multiple courses, and they are still quite interested in our careers, taking some pride in our successes (well . . . that is . . . before this book was published).